UNITED STATES DEPARTMENT OF THE INTERIOR

STRATEGIC PLAN
FOR FISCAL YEARS
2014 – 2018

I0439851

CONTENTS

LETTER FROM THE SECRETARY

I am pleased to present the Department of the Interior's Strategic Plan for FY 2014-2018. The DOI's broad mission responsibilities span the Nation, from the Arctic in Alaska to the southern tip of Florida, and from Midway Island in the Pacific Ocean to the Virgin Islands in the Caribbean. We manage 500 million acres of lands primarily located in the western states and 1.7 billion acres on the Outer Continental Shelf. The activities of DOI are an economic engine. In 2012, DOI's programs contributed an estimated $371 billion to the U.S. economy and supported 2.3 million jobs in activities including outdoor recreation and tourism, energy development, grazing and timber harvesting.[1]

The DOI's programs contribute to the quality of life for many people and communities across the Country and help to advance goals for stewardship and energy independence. Nearly every American lives within an hour's drive of lands or waters managed by DOI. In 2012, there were 417 million visits to DOI managed lands. Recreational visits to DOI's lands had an economic benefit to local communities, particularly in rural areas, contributing an estimated $45 billion in economic activity in 2012. The DOI oversees the responsible development of 23 percent of U.S. energy supplies, is the largest supplier and manager of water in the 17 Western States, maintains relationships with 566 federally recognized tribes, and provides services to more than 1.7 million American Indian and Alaska Native peoples.

The context for this Plan reflects the complex mission of DOI and how it affects the lives of all Americans. The DOI's 70,000 employees work in partnership with other Federal agencies, states, tribes, industry, and a rich diversity of stakeholders to preserve and interpret the Nation's rich heritage and history; manage diverse Federal lands, waters, and wildlife and fishery resources; provide world-class science that protects us from hazards and provides the public with critical information on the earth, energy, water, and resource conservation; ensure the conservation and delivery of water for diverse users; and deliver a suite of programs for American Indian and Insular communities.

Developed with input from our stakeholders, the Plan demonstrates how we integrate and align diverse and geographically dispersed programs and projects to effectively and efficiently deliver services to the American public.

Effective management of DOI requires dynamic and modern strategies to confront major trends including the likelihood of continued and increasingly constrained funding resources, the changing demographics of the population that is becoming more urban, diverse, and technologically advanced, and a changing climate that will continue to have impacts on land, water, wildlife, and tribal communities.

In early FY 2014, I realigned DOI's strategic goals to guide and focus DOI's efforts in FY 2014 and beyond. The Plan presents these priorities in 6 mission areas that capture responsibilities administered by 10 bureaus and multiple offices.

---

[1] U.S. Department of the Interior Economic Report FY 2012; July 29, 2013; available at http://www.doi.gov/ppa/economic_analysis/upload/FY2012-DOI-Econ-Report-Final-2013-09-25.pdf

- <u>Celebrating and Enhancing America's Great Outdoors</u>. The DOI's efforts included in this mission area foster the intrinsic link between healthy economies and healthy landscapes with goals and strategies to increase tourism and outdoor recreation in balance with preservation and conservation. Collaborative and community-driven efforts and outcome-focused investments will focus on preserving and enhancing rural landscapes, urban parks and rivers, important ecosystems, cultural resources, and wildlife habitat. The goals and strategies incorporate the best available science, a landscape-level understanding, and stakeholder input to identify and share conservation priorities.

- <u>Strengthening Tribal Nations</u>. The goals and strategies build upon progress made over the past 4 years to establish strong and meaningful relationships with tribes, strengthen the government-to-government relationships, deliver services to American Indians and Alaska Natives, and advance self-governance and self-determination. The DOI efforts in this mission area restore tribal homelands, fulfill commitments for Indian water rights, develop energy resources, expand educational opportunities, and assist in the management of climate change.

- <u>Powering Our Future and Responsible Use of Our Resources</u>. The DOI plays a significant role in the President's all-of-the-above energy strategy to secure an energy future for the Nation that is cleaner and more sustainable The goals and strategies take a landscape-level approach to energy development, modernizing programs and practices, improving transparency, streamlining permitting, and strengthening inspection and enforcement.

- <u>Engaging the Next Generation</u>. To address the growing disconnect between young people and the outdoors, the goals and strategies in this area to promote public-private partnerships and collaborative efforts across all levels of government to connect young people with the land and inspire them to play, learn, serve, and work outdoors. The DOI efforts encompassed by the goals and strategies include the 21st Century Conservation Service Corps to leverage public investment and private philanthropy to build job skills, improve national parks and public lands, create opportunities for veterans, and create connections to the land for the next generation.

- <u>Ensuring Healthy Watersheds and Sustainable, Secure Water Supplies</u>. The DOI's efforts in this mission area recognize the importance of water as the foundation for healthy communities and healthy economies and the challenges resulting from climate change, drought conditions, and increasing demand. The goals and strategies position the Department to work with states in managing water resources, raising awareness and support for sustainable water usage, maintaining critical infrastructure, promoting efficiency and conservation, supporting healthy rivers and streams, and restoring key ecosystems.

- <u>Building a Landscape-Level Understanding of Our Resources</u>. This mission area includes DOI's efforts to harness existing and emerging technologies and elevate understanding of resources on a landscape-level by advancing knowledge in the fields of ecosystem services and resilience, energy and mineral resource assessments, hazard response and mitigation, water security, sacred sites, climate change adaptation, and environmental health. Landscape-level approaches to management hold the promise of a broader based and more consistent consideration of development and conservation. This mission area includes goals and strategies that advance this approach including applied and basic scientific research and the development of science products to inform decisionmaking by DOI's bureaus and offices and local, state, national, and international communities. The DOI's science agency, the U.S. Geological Survey, generates essential scientific information and data that is used as the basis for decisionmaking, including earth observation satellite imagery and stream gage and seismic data. The DOI leverages its role as the managing partner for the National Geospatial Platform to turn vast amounts of data into usable information and advance broader-based and more consistent landscape and resource management, aligning the scientific programs to complement each other and other agencies to better support the Nation's research and development priorities.

This Strategic Plan presents our vision, emphasizing the areas where we will focus our efforts over the next 4 years and allow the American public to hold us accountable. The Plan complies with the Government Performance and Results Modernization Act of 2010, presenting the goals, strategies, and performance measures that will be used by DOI's employees to achieve desired outcomes and evaluate the performance of contributing programs and their personal performance. The Plan informs our actions, guides resource allocations, and is the basis to assess progress and inform the public about our priorities.

You will note that the Plan is reformatted to more clearly present our principles and focal areas. A new section in the Plan, *Highlighted Initiatives to Achieve Secretarial Priorities*, displays detailed action plans for achievement of goals in each of the mission areas. This section includes DOI's Agency Priority Goals that track with Presidential commitments as reported on www.performance.gov. To complement the Plan, the DOI's Annual Performance Plan and Report will accompany the President's budget to identify annual performance increments, funding investments consistent with DOI's program inventory, and a comprehensive assessment of performance across all the mission areas with trend data for prior years.

I hope you will read the Plan and follow our progress in the Annual Performance Plan and Report as we continue to work toward accomplishment of the ambitious goals we have set for DOI. You can follow our progress on www.doi.gov or www.performance.gov.

Sincerely,

Sally Jewell

MISSION AND ORGANIZATION

Mission

The DOI protects and manages the Nation's natural resources and cultural heritage; provides scientific and other information about those resources; and honors the Nation's trust responsibilities or special commitments to American Indians, Alaska Natives, and affiliated island communities.

History

In 1849 President Polk signed the bill creating the Home Department. The DOI was charged with managing a wide variety of programs, which included overseeing Indian Affairs, exploring the western wilderness, directing the District of Columbia jail, constructing the National Capital's water system, managing hospitals and universities, improving historic western emigrant routes, marking boundaries, issuing patents, conducting the census, and researching the geological resources of the United States. As the Country matured during the last half of the 19th Century, so did the Department and its mission began to evolve as some of these functions moved to other agencies.

Surface Lands Managed by the Department of the Interior

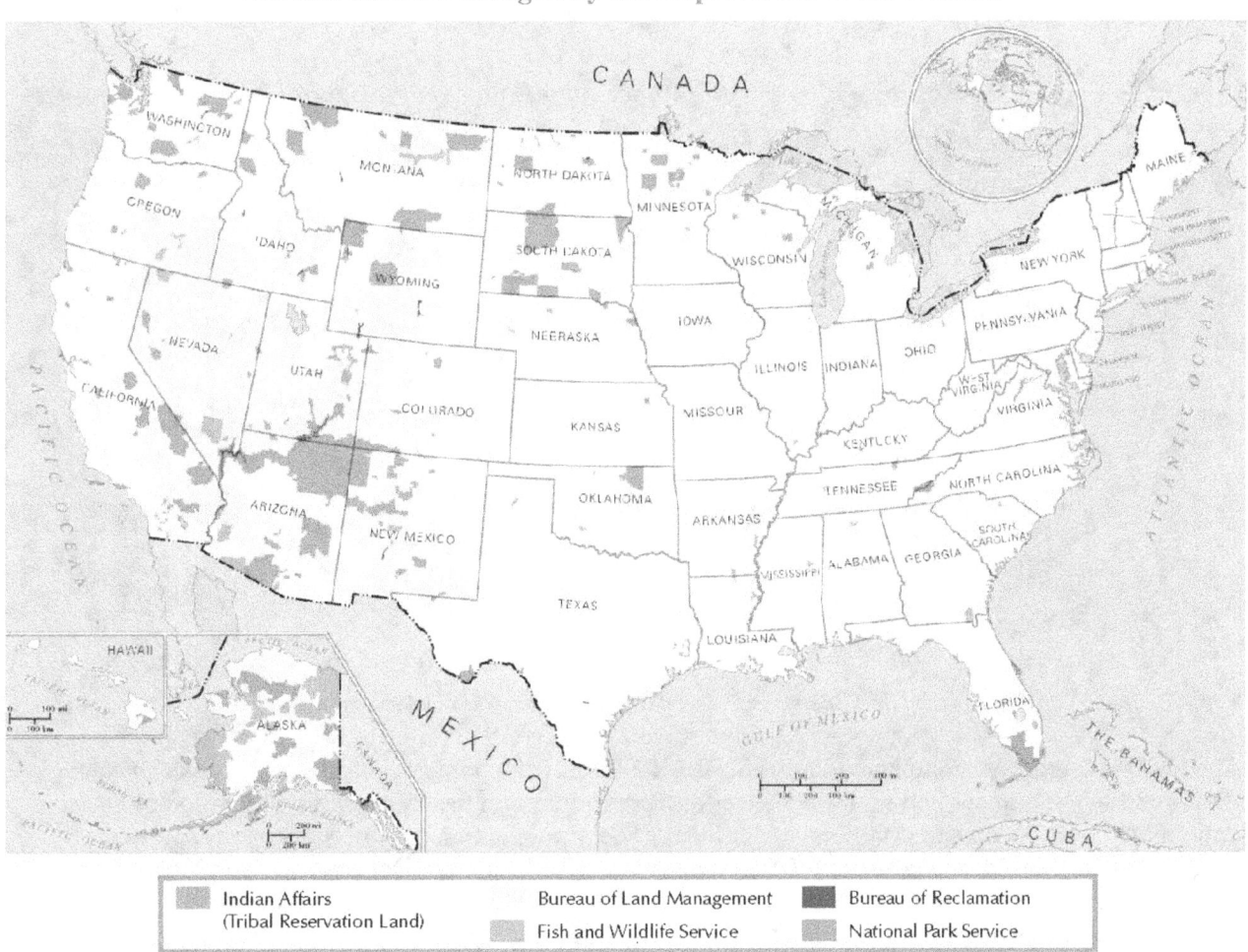

Indian Affairs (Tribal Reservation Land)	Bureau of Land Management	Bureau of Reclamation
	Fish and Wildlife Service	National Park Service

Following Theodore Roosevelt's conservation summit and the conservation movement at the beginning of the 20th Century, there was an increasing urgency and expanding congressional mandate to protect and more effectively manage the Country's natural resources. Accordingly, DOI's mission shifted to focus on the preservation, management, understanding, and use of public lands, natural and cultural resources, responsible management of energy and water resources, and responsibilities related to Indian nations and scientific discovery.

Today, DOI manages the Nation's public lands and minerals, including providing access to more than 500 million acres of public lands, 700 million acres of subsurface minerals, and 1.7 billion acres of the Outer Continental Shelf. The DOI is the steward of 20 percent of the Nation's lands, including national parks, national wildlife refuges, and public lands; manages resources that supply 23 percent of the Nation's energy; supplies and manages water in the 17 Western States and supplies 17 percent of the Nation's hydropower energy; and upholds Federal trust responsibilities to 566 federally recognized Indian tribes and Alaska Natives. The DOI is responsible for migratory bird and wildlife conservation; historic preservation; endangered species conservation; surface-mined lands protection and restoration; mapping, geological, hydrological, and biological science for the Nation; and financial and technical assistance for the insular areas.

United States Continental Shelf Boundary Areas

Robert Utley and Barry Mackintosh, *The Department of Everything Else: Highlights of Interior History*, 1988, pp. 1-2.

The DOI's programs encompassed in this Strategic Plan cover a broad spectrum of activities that are performed by 10 bureaus and multiple offices and are captured in the following presentation of each entity's unique mission and set of responsibilities. The Strategic Plan's 6 mission areas capture the vitality, inventiveness, and potential of the bureaus and offices and the Department's 70,000 dedicated and skilled employees. Along with employees, almost 280,000 volunteers contribute their time in support of bureau and office missions, bringing unique local knowledge to park operations, assisting in recovery from natural disasters, and participating in environmental education, among other activities.

U.S. Department of the Interior Organization

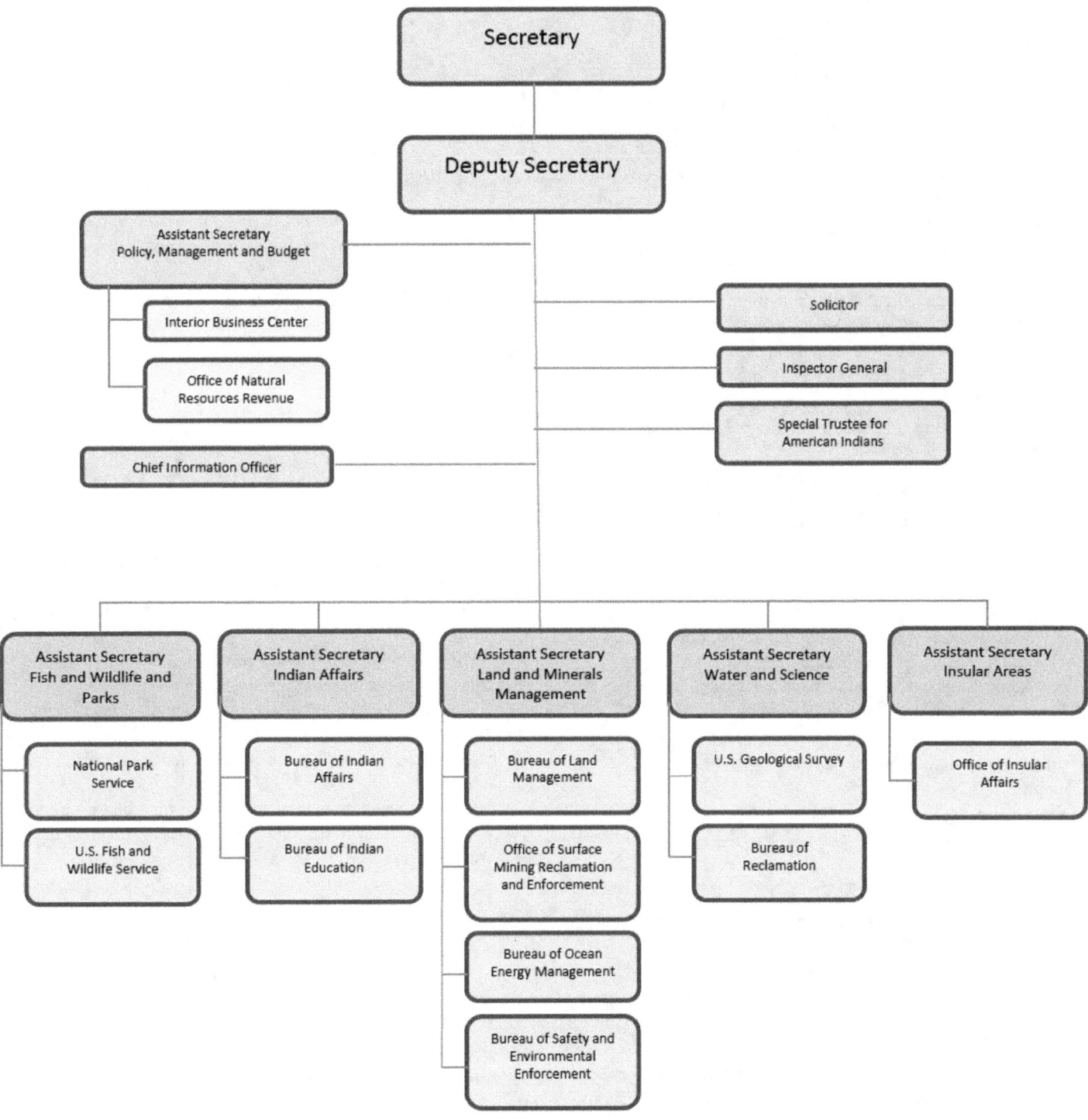

Bureau and Office Summary

Bureau of Land Management (BLM)

▶ Manages and conserves resources for multiple use and sustained yield on approximately 248 million acres of public land, and an additional 700 million acres of subsurface federal mineral estate, including the following:

▷ Renewable and conventional energy and mineral development

▷ Forest management, timber and biomass production

▷ Wild Horse and Burro management

▷ Management of diverse landscapes for the benefit of wildlife, domestic grazing, and recreational uses

▷ Resource management at sites of natural, scenic, scientific, and historical value including the National Landscape Conservation System

Bureau of Ocean Energy Management (BOEM)

▶ Manages access to renewable and conventional energy resources of the Outer Continental Shelf (OCS)

▶ Administers over 6,400 active fluid mineral leases on approximately 35 million OCS acres

▶ Issues leases that provide 24 percent of domestic crude oil and eight percent of domestic natural gas supply.

▶ Oversees lease and grant issuance for off-shore renewable energy projects

Bureau of Safety and Environmental Enforcement (BSEE)

▶ Promotes safety, protects the environment, and conserves resources offshore through regulatory enforcement of offshore oil and gas facilities on the 1.7 billion acre US Outer Continental Shelf (OCS)

▶ Oversees oil spill for US facilities in state and federal waters and operates the Ohmsett National Oil Spill Response Research test facility

▶ Supports research to promote the use of best available safest technology for oil spill response

Office of Surface Mining Reclamation and Enforcement (OSMRE)

▶ Protects the environment during coal mining through Federal programs, provides grants to states and tribes, and oversight activities

▶ Ensures the land is reclaimed afterwards

▶ Mitigates the effects of past mining by pursuing reclamation of abandoned coal mine lands

U.S. Geological Survey (USGS)

▶ Conducts scientific research in ecosystems, climate and land use change, mineral assessments, environmental health, and water resources to inform effective decision making and planning

▶ Produces information to increase understanding of natural hazards such as earthquakes, volcanoes, and landslides

▶ Conducts research on oil, gas, and alternative energy potential, production, consumption, and environmental effects

▶ Leads the effort on climate change science research for the Department

▶ Provides access to natural science information to support decisions about how to respond to natural risks and manage natural resources

Bureau of Reclamation (BOR)

▶ Manages, develops, and protects water and related resources in an environmentally and economically sound manner in the interest of the American public

▶ Largest wholesale supplier of water in the Nation

▶ Manages 476 dams and 337 reservoirs

▶ Delivers water to 1 in every 5 western farmers and more than 31 million people

▶ America's second largest producer of hydroelectric power

Fish and Wildlife Service (FWS)

▶ Manages the 150 million-acre National Wildlife Refuge System primarily for the benefit of fish and wildlife

▶ Manages 70 fish hatcheries and other related facilities for endangered species recovery and to restore native fisheries populations

▶ Protects and conserves:
  ▷ Migratory birds
  ▷ Threatened and endangered species
  ▷ Certain marine mammals

▶ Hosts approximately 47 million visitors annually at 561 refuges located in all 50 states and 38 wetland management districts

National Park Service (NPS)

▶ Maintains and manages a network of 401 natural, cultural, and recreational sites for the benefit and enjoyment of the American people

▶ Manages and protects over 26,000 historic structures, over 44 million acres of designated wilderness, and a wide range of museum collections and cultural and natural landscapes

▶ Provides outdoor recreation to over 286 million annual park visitors

▶ Provides technical assistance and support to state and local natural and cultural resource sites and programs, and fulfills responsibilities under the National Historic Preservation Act

Indian Affairs (IA)

▶ Fulfills Indian trust responsibilities
▶ Promotes self-determination on behalf of 566 federally recognized Indian tribes
▶ Funds compacts and contracts to support natural resource education, law enforcement, and social service programs that are delivered by tribes
▶ Operates 182 elementary and secondary schools and dormitories, providing educational services to 42,000 students in 23 states
▶ Supports 29 tribally controlled community colleges, universities, and post-secondary schools
Note: IA includes the Bureau of Indian Affairs and the Bureau of Indian Education

Departmental Offices

▶ Immediate Office of the Secretary and Assistant Secretaries
▶ Policy, Management and Budget provides leadership and support for the following:
  ▷ Budget, Finance, Performance and Acquisition
  ▷ Public Safety, Resource Protection and Emergency Services
  ▷ Natural Resources Revenue Management
  ▷ Human Capital and Diversity
  ▷ Technology, Information and Business Services
  ▷ Policy and International Affairs
  ▷ Natural Resource Damage Assessment
  ▷ Wildland Fire Management
  ▷ Central Hazardous Materials Management
▶ Office of Inspector General
▶ Office of the Solicitor
▶ Office of the Special Trustee for American Indians
▶ Assistant Secretary for Insular Areas and the Office of Insular Affairs

DEPARTMENT-WIDE PRINCIPLES

The DOI operates based on a set of key principles and tenets that guide the efforts of 70,000 employees, volunteers, and other stakeholders that deliver a broad spectrum of services and programs. These principles serve as the standard of operations throughout DOI and ensure achievement of the highest of ideals while performing the mission.

Stewards of the Nation's Natural, Cultural, and Heritage Assets

The DOI is committed to being an outstanding steward of approximately 500 million acres of public lands and 700 million subsurface acres including magnificent vistas, unique ecosystems, and treasured natural, cultural, and heritage assets. The management and oversight of these resources require a dedicated cadre of employees, the contributions of volunteers, and the input of stakeholders to inform decision making. The challenges of managing for a diverse constituency while meeting national goals for energy development and sustaining high levels of recreation and access require technical expertise, the best available science, and a landscape-level understanding of the balance of development and conservation.

Effective and Efficient Operations

The DOI is committed to achieving effective and efficient management. Executives and managers rely extensively on collaboration and partnerships that leverage resources. The DOI utilizes an extensive framework of internal controls to protect against fraud and waste and implements recommendations from the Government Accountability Office and the Office of Inspector General. On an annual basis, DOI reviews program activities for opportunities to eliminate lower priority programs, re-engineer under-

Department of the Interior Headquarters, Washington, DC

achieving programs, and investigate new ideas to increase the effectiveness and efficiency of program delivery. Through the President's SAVE awards program and other efforts that incentivize creative cost cutting, DOI is focused on specific management initiatives, which are described in greater detail in the Appendix.

Financial Integrity and Transparency

The DOI is committed to effective financial operations and accountability including high quality and timely reporting, robust internal controls, clean audits, and effective follow-up on audit and internal control findings. The DOI utilizes the Financial and Business Management System for the integration of business functions including budget execution, finance, acquisition, and others with single sign on, improved internal controls, a secure information technology environment, and a community of business innovation, efficiency, and transparency.

Ensuring High Ethical Standards

Key to maintaining public trust and confidence in the integrity of government is the adherence of high ethical standards and ensuring that government business is conducted with impartiality and integrity. The DOI embodies this principle, follows the law and holds people accountable. Accountability is a key theme – DOI expects to be held accountable. The DOI does not tolerate lapses that detract and distract from good, honest service to the American people. Decisions are based on sound science and the best interest of the public. The Department promotes and supports transparency, accountability, and efficiency.

Making DOI the Best and Most Inclusive Place to Work in America

The DOI is committed to making the Department the best and most inclusive place to work. Changing demographics of the population, generational shifts, increased urbanization, and increased use of technology makes the management of a changing cadre of employees challenging. The DOI will foster an environment that is open and accepting of individual differences and encourages employees to maximize their potential and to provide quality public service. The DOI will ensure that policies, practices, and systems do not benefit any one group over another and that the differences that each employee brings to the Department are respected and can enhance the organization's capacity, service, and adaptability.

Safety, Security, Preparedness, Response, and Recovery

One of DOI's top priorities is to focus on safety, security, and preparedness activities. The DOI will uphold its responsibilities for protecting lives, resources, property, and the environment through a wide variety of program areas, including law enforcement, health and safety, security, aviation, environmental compliance and emergency management. The DOI will provide technical expertise and capability for interagency preparedness, response and recovery activities as defined in Presidential Policy Directive 8 and the five National Frameworks (Protection, Prevention, Response, Recovery, and Mitigation), and as required by other interagency plans such as the *National Oil and Hazardous Substance Pollution Contingency Plan*. The DOI resources are frequently called upon for wildland fire and oil spill response, public works and engineering activities, search and rescue operations, protection of natural and cultural resources and historic properties expertise, rebuilding after storm and hazard events, and law enforcement missions. Interior has the third largest contingent of Federal law enforcement officers in the Executive Branch with 3,500 officers that patrol vast acres of federal lands, national parks, wildlife refuges, and Indian communities. To ensure DOI is prepared to meet its preparedness, response, and recovery obligations, the Department and Bureaus maintain plans for all-hazards to safeguard the environment.

Respecting Tribal Self-Governance

The DOI recognizes the importance of the nation-to-nation relationship with tribes and will continue to encourage tribal management of resources and self-determination; consultation and support for effective management of the tribal trust; and the need to uphold commitments to tribes and Indian communities. Building coalitions will be an important aspect of these principles, including respect for the viewpoints of the 566 Indian tribes and the importance of maintaining strong tribal communities.

Consultation is a key component of respecting Tribal self-governance and supporting the nation-to-nation relationship. The DOI upholds the principles set forth in the President's *Executive Order 13175 Consultation and Coordination with Indian Tribal Governments*. All of DOI's bureaus and offices operate under a policy consistent with the Executive Order that considers the impacts of policies, processes, rulemaking, and legislation regarding tribes and tribal communities.

International Engagement and Leadership

The DOI participates in the United States' efforts to address climate change; protect biodiversity; sustainably manage energy, water, and natural resources; empower indigenous communities; protect cultural heritage; and ensure sound science as the basis for decisionmaking. The resources for which DOI is responsible cross jurisdictional boundaries and DOI is a key player in the international community confronting the exploitation of natural resources, trade in wildlife, spread of invasive species, the arctic, and a multiplicity of scientific issues. The DOI is committed to maintaining its relevance and will engage in international efforts as a core mission responsibility, consistent with its unique expertise and mandate.

Increasing Climate Change Preparedness and Resilience

The DOI's responsibilities for management of lands, waters, and wildlife provide first-hand experience of the impacts of a rapidly changing climate. Impacts observed by Federal resource managers include drought, severe flooding, interrupted pollination of crops, changes in wildlife and prey behavior, warmer rivers and streams, and sea level rise. The DOI will bring the best science to bear to understand these consequences and will undertake mitigation, adaptation, and enhancements to support natural resilience and will take steps to reduce carbon pollution, including through the responsible development of clean energy. The DOI will be a national leader in integrating preparedness and resilience efforts into its mission areas, goals, strategies, and programs; identifying vulnerabilities and systematically addressing these vulnerabilities; and incorporating climate change strategies into management plans, policies, programs, and operations.

CLIMATE CHANGE - THE DEPARTMENT OF THE INTERIOR

The DOI is committed to adaptively manage resources to mitigate the impacts of climate change, consider climate change on a landscape-level to improve resiliency, and work across agency lines to develop and provide data, information and decision support tools. The Strategic Plan utilizes goals, strategies, and metrics that support DOI's integrated approach to climate change as demonstrated by the following examples:

MISSION AREA #1 CELEBRATING AND ENHANCING AMERICA'S GREAT OUTDOORS
Climate change can act as a stressor and impacts efforts to protect America's landscapes, sustain fish and wildlife species, and protect cultural and heritage resources. The occurrence of wildland fire is exacerbated by the effects of climate change. Fire managers implement a comprehensive strategy that aligns Federal, state, tribal, and local efforts in preparedness, suppression, hazardous fuels reduction, and habitat restoration programs that consider the impacts of climate change.

MISSION AREA #2 STRENGTHENING TRIBAL NATIONS AND INSULAR COMMUNITIES
Climate change has a particular impact on American Indians and Alaska Natives that rely on resources for subsistence and economic development. The Strategic Plan includes goals, strategies and measures to gage the effective management of agriculture, grazing, timber, hunting, and fishing. The DOI resource managers consider the impacts of climate change in the management of these programs.

MISSION AREA #3 POWERING OUR FUTURE AND RESPONSIBLE USE OF THE NATION'S RESOURCES
The DOI's Strategic Plan includes goals, strategies and metrics that promote the development of energy and sustainable management of timber, forage, and non-energy minerals. Climate change is a factor that is considered in the planning and management of resources for utilization of energy, timber, and forage.

MISSION AREA #4 ENGAGING THE NEXT GENERATION
The DOI is committed to increasing the engagement of youth as active stewards of the environment and to promote youth employment, education, community service, and volunteerism. The DOI Strategic Plan include goals and strategies to gage performance of these efforts, which incorporate activities focused on climate change.

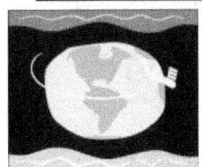

MISSION AREA #5 ENSURING HEALTHY WATERSHEDS AND SUSTAINABLE, SECURE WATER SUPPLIES
Water is a precious commodity that is increasingly impacted by climate change. The DOI's strategies for healthy watersheds and sustainable water supplies considers these impacts, promoting water conservation and partnerships for the responsible management of water supplies.

MISSION AREA #6 BUILDING A LANDSCAPE-LEVEL UNDERSTANDING OF OUR RESOURCES

The DOI is committed to assessing climate change impacts on a landscape scale, incorporating collaborative approaches and leveraging efforts with others to inform decisionmaking. The DOI Strategic Plan includes goals and strategies that promote data availability and use, leveraging the DOI's role in management of the geospatial platform.

Throughout the performance of its mission areas, DOI is a responsible steward for the significant land, water, and wildlife resources for which DOI is entrusted. The DOI has an obligation to ensure the sustainability of its own operations to promote energy efficiency and reduce greenhouse gases and the carbon footprint. The Strategic Plan promotes fulfillment of DOI's commitment to these efforts reducing its potential contributions to the causes of climate change.

HIGHLIGHTED INITIATIVES FOR ACHIEVING SECRETARIAL PRIORITIES

The following initiatives are highlighted as select activities considered particularly important to help fulfill the priorities that have been identified by the Secretary of the Interior. While this list is not all inclusive of the full range of activities being conducted throughout the DOI, these are identified to provide emphasis on select programmatic initiatives that are considered to play significant roles in furthering the DOI mission over the timeframe of this Strategic Plan (FY 2014-2018) especially for those priority areas identified by the Secretary in her letter. These highlighted initiatives have been arranged according to the corresponding mission areas and strategic goals which are more fully discussed later in the Plan. Embedded within the set of initiatives are the DOI's "Agency" Priority Performance Goals that are further highlighted in www.performance.gov.

MISSION AREA #1 CELEBRATING AND ENHANCING AMERICA'S GREAT OUTDOORS

Protect America's Landscapes and Species: Initiatives under this goal protect and restore America's large landscapes; conserve and restore wildlife populations; and improve efforts to manage lands and resources for resiliency.

- Climate change and resilience
  - Incorporate climate change projections into analyses of resource threats, trends, data, and monitoring needs, future planning needs, and other resource needs of National park Service foundational planning documents.
  - Increase climate change resiliency and green infrastructure by implementing 30 storm mitigation projects in the Northeast and work collaboratively to prioritize science driven restoration projects to conserve the Gulf of Mexico watershed.
  - Climate Change Priority Goal: Understand, communicate, and respond to the diversity of impacts associated with climate change across the various landscapes of the United States. By September 30, 2015, the DOI will demonstrate maturing implementation of climate change adaptation as scored when carrying out strategies in its Strategic Sustainability Performance Plan.
- Conserve sage-grouse
  - Conserve Greater Sage-Grouse and the sagebrush ecosystem it occupies by amending or revising Resource Management Plans and implementing restoration actions that address the needs of the sage-grouse.
- Restore the Everglades
  - Restore the quantity, quality, timing, and distribution of water to the Everglades; preserve and restore native Everglades habitats and species; and foster compatibility of built and natural systems in and affecting the Everglades by:
    - Initiating efforts to plan for and construct the Tamiami Trail 2.6-Mile Bridge in cooperation with the State of Florida and others.
    - Initiating development of an operations plan for the Modified Water Deliveries Project to provide more natural water delivery to Everglades National Park.
    - Developing a framework for detection and early response to invasive exotic species.
- Restore bison populations
  - Restore and sustain three ranging bison populations in collaboration with states, tribes, private landowners, and other public land management agencies in:
    - Great Sand Dunes National Park/Preserve and Baca National Wildlife Refuge in southern Colorado
    - Badlands National Park South Unit on the Pine Ridge Reservation in South Dakota
    - Public and State lands near Grand Canyon National Park in Arizona

- Combat wildlife trafficking
  - o Finalize and begin implementation of the National Strategy for Combating Wildlife Trafficking, in cooperation with the Departments of State and Justice.

Protect America's Cultural and Heritage Resources: Initiatives will advance historic preservation and understanding of the Nation's heritage.
- Prepare for the NPS Centennial
  - o Improve the condition of 469 of the National Park Service highest priority facilities in preparation for the NPS Centennial in 2016.
- Enhance historic preservation
  - o Complete implementation of the Report on the Federal Historic Preservation Tax Incentives Program recommendations to promote economic development and community revitalization, especially in urban areas.
- Enhance management of Indian cultural interests
  - o Develop a revised FWS Native American Policy in collaboration with tribal representatives from across the Nation.
  - o Finalize a rule to allow members of federally recognized Indian tribes to gather plants and minerals for traditional cultural purposes within units of the National Park System.

Enhance Recreation and Visitor Experience: Initiatives will improve outdoor recreation access and increase opportunities for public enjoyment of Federal lands, waters, and shorelines, and help connect urban populations to parks and green spaces.
- Recreation on public lands
  - o Develop a strategy to expand recreational opportunities on national wildlife refuges, BLM conservation lands, and national parks.
- Urban Recreation
  - o Increase the number of close-to-home outdoor recreational and wellness programs:
    - ▪ Facilitate 300 or more community-led natural resource conservation and outdoor recreation projects in over 800 communities.
    - ▪ Increase the number of Urban Wildlife Refuge Partnerships.

MISSION AREA #2 STRENGTHENING TRIBAL NATIONS AND INSULAR COMMUNITIES

Initiatives will improve the nation-to-nation relationships with tribes and fulfill the United States' trust responsibilities through partnerships to build stronger economies and safer Indian communities.
- Safer and More Resilient Communities in Indian Country Priority Goal: Reduce repeat incarceration in Indian Communities. By September 30, 2015, reduce rates of repeat incarceration in 3 target tribal communities by 3 percent through a comprehensive "alternatives to incarceration" strategy that seeks to address underlying causes of repeat offenses, including substance abuse and social service needs through tribal and federal partnerships.
- Economic opportunity
  - o Promote economic opportunity by converting 500,000 acres from fee to trust.

MISSION AREA #3 POWERING OUR FUTURE AND RESPONSIBLE USE OF THE NATION'S RESOURCES

Initiatives will promote responsible development of domestic energy resources.
- Ensure environmental compliance and safety
  - o Finalize OSMRE's Stream Protection Rule, BOEM/BSEE Alaska standards, and BSEE Production Safety Rule and Blowout Preventer Rule.
  - o Modernize offshore leasing and diligence requirements for deepwater Gulf of Mexico.

- Develop renewable energy potential
  - Renewable Energy Priority Goal: Increase the approved capacity for production of energy from domestic renewable resources to support a growing economy and protect our national interests while reducing our dependence on foreign oil and climate changing greenhouse gas emissions. By September 30, 2015, increase approved capacity authorized for renewable solar, wind, and geothermal energy resources affecting DOI managed lands while ensuring full environmental review to at least 16,500 megawatts (since 2009) Conduct lease sales offshore MD, NJ, and MA in 2014; facilitate expanded research and demonstration activities offshore NC, OR, and HI; and review proposals for development of the Atlantic Wind Connect's transmission backbone project.
  - Improve hydropower plant efficiency with software upgrades, new turbines, and pumping station operation flexibility.
- Responsibly develop conventional energy potential
  - Automate onshore Application for Permit to Drill tracking and processing.
  - Develop ePlans and ePermits for offshore exploration and development.
  - Develop and publish the Outer Continental Shelf Oil and Gas Leasing Program for 2017-2022.
- Manage energy production and revenue
  - Finalize the Hydraulic Fracturing Rule, Onshore Order 9 (waste prevention, venting, and flaring), and revisions to onshore oil and gas royalty rates.
  - Oil and Gas Development Priority Goal: Improve production accountability, safety, and environmental protection of oil and gas operations through increased inspection of high-risk oil and gas production cases. By September 30, 2015, BLM will increase the completion of inspections of federal and Indian high-risk oil and gas cases by nine percent over 2011 levels, which is equivalent to covering as much as 95 percent of the potential high risk cases.

MISSION AREA #4 ENGAGING THE NEXT GENERATION

Initiatives will promote the engagement of young people as active stewards of the environment.

- Play:
  - Develop or enhance outdoor recreation partnerships in a total of 50 cities to create new, systemic opportunities for outdoor play for over 10 million young people.
- Learn:
  - Provide educational opportunities to at least 10 million of the Nation's K-12 student population annually.
- Serve:
  - Attain 1,000,000 volunteers annually on public lands.
- Work:
  - Youth Employment and Training Priority Goal: Build the next generation of conservation and community leaders by supporting youth employment at the DOI. By September 30, 2015, the DOI will provide 40,000 work & training opportunities over two fiscal years, 2014 and 2015, for individuals ages 15 to 25 to support the mission of the DOI.

MISSION AREA #5 ENSURING HEALTHY WATERSHEDS AND SUSTAINABLE, SECURE WATER SUPPLIES

Manage Water and Watersheds for the 21st Century: Initiatives will support reliable delivery of water for multiple purposes, help balance competing water resource goals, and build collaborative partnerships with Federal and non-Federal stakeholders.

- Basin studies
  - Complete 17 basin studies to develop strategies for managing watersheds, including adapting to the effects of climate change.

- California water resources
  - Complete CALFED feasibility storage studies for potential enlargement of two major California river basins (Shasta and Upper San Joaquin) while continuing work on other storage studies, and begin San Joaquin River construction projects addressing water supply and fishery needs.
- Colorado River basin management
  - Publish a draft Environmental Impact Statement for the Colorado River Basin long term experimental and management plan.
  - Extend the current five-year Colorado River Basin agreement by renegotiating and implementing "Minute 319" and implemented related drought strategies.
- Restore urban rivers
  - Promote the current eighteen pilot locations of the Urban Water Federal Partnership and examine ways to strengthen the existing program and provide additional opportunities to other cities and towns as appropriate.
- Manage water and related resources in the Columbia River
  - Provide support for Columbia River negotiations.
  - Support elements of the Yakima Basin Integrated Plan that are cost-effective and have a strong Federal interest.
- Elwha River
  - Create an adaptive management decision support tool for Elwha River Restoration.
- USGS National Water Census and Environmental Flows
  - Provide data to inform decisions on water delivery for multiple use

Extend Water Supplies Through Conservation: The WaterSmart (Sustain and Manage America's Resources for Tomorrow) program assists communities in stretching water supplies while improving water management and increasing the efficient use of water.

- Enable water conservation capability

  Water Conservation Priority Goal: Enable capability to increase the available water supply in the western States through conservation-related programs to ensure adequate and safe water supplies By September 30, 2015, the DOI will further enable the capability to increase the available water supply for agricultural, municipal, industrial, and environmental uses in the western United States through Reclamation water conservation programs to 840,000 acre-feet, cumulatively since the end of 2009

Enhance Availability of Water to Tribal Communities: The Department ensures the availability of water to tribal nations by implementing Indian water rights settlements, providing technical assistance to tribes, and undertaking tribal ecosystem restoration and rural water projects consistent with the goal of strengthening tribal nations.

- Indian water settlements
  - Work to finalize settlements where issues are close to resolution. Implement a long-term strategy for improving federal engagement and bringing greater certainty to settlement negotiations and implementation.
  - Begin water deliveries to Navajo Nation through the Navajo Gallup Water Supply Project.

MISSION AREA #6 BUILDING A LANDSCAPE-LEVEL UNDERSTANDING OF OUR RESOURCES

Provide Shared Landscape-Level Management and Planning Tools: Initiatives will leverage data and capability to improve decision making.

- Geospatial Platform
  - Develop high priority landscape-level applications in the areas of climate resilience, ecosystem restoration, and sustainable resource management.
- Landsat Data and Science
  - Provide biological carbon sequestration capacity for the lower 48 states, Alaska, and Hawaii through a visualization tool.
  - Make available Nationwide natural resource management products for wildfire burned area, surface water extent, and snow covered area.
  - Update the National Land Cover Database 30-meter resolution information on urban, agriculture, forested, and impervious areas, including tree canopy.
- Inventory and Monitoring
  - Make Fish & Wildlife Service Inventory and Monitoring Program data available to partners, state and local governments, academia, and other resource management groups, to further conservation efforts .
  - Complete BLM Rapid Eco-regional assessments including integrating shrub and grassland vegetation monitoring protocols and survey strategy with the Natural Resource Conservation Service.
  - Complete the Tennessee Land Unsuitability Petition for mining.

Provide Science to Understand, Model, and Predict Ecosystem, Climate, and Land Use Change: Initiatives will assist Federal, state, local, and tribal entities by monitoring water quality and quantity; analyzing energy and mineral resources potential and environmental effects of their extraction and use; and analyze and monitor changes to the land and ocean environments.

- Mississippi River
  - Update the Nutrient transport/transformation model for the Mississippi River Basin (SPARROW) to reduce hypoxia in the Gulf of Mexico.
- Sacramento- San Joaquin River Delta
  - Produce a 3-D Geologic Framework and Seismic Velocity Model for use across the Sacramento- San Joaquin River Delta.
- Chesapeake Bay
  - Assess water quality and wildlife including: factors affecting health of fisheries, ground water-quality and conditions resulting from management actions, effects of hydro-geochemical processes on water nutrients and quality, biogenic duck habitat model and effects of toxic contaminants on fish-eating birds, and combined effects of land and climate change on streamflow.
- Sage Grouse
  - Support Landscape Science and Conservation planning providing:
    - Evaluation of the impacts of energy development on sage grouse.
    - Better understanding the threat of altered fire regimes, spread of invasive plants, and climate change.
    - Analysis of population and habitat connectivity.
    - Updating geospatial mapping of sagebrush landscape.
    - Developing a comprehensive database of research and monitoring data.
- DOI Climate Science Centers (CSC)
  - Complete an ecosystem model to understand climate impacts on Alaskan natural resources.
  - Integrate scenarios for future climate, hydrology, and vegetation for the Northwest.
  - Assess climate sensitive ecosystems in the Southeastern US.
  - Develop regional drought impact scenarios for the North Central and South Central CSC's to facilitate planning of adaptation actions.

Provide Scientific Data to Protect, Instruct and Inform Communities: The USGS will lead the scientific research on the environment and natural hazards and provide information to partners and stakeholders for use in making decisions that will protect lives.

- Coastal resiliency
  - Update forecasts of erosion vulnerability to hurricanes for the Gulf and Atlantic Coasts including topography and bathymetry, analysis of shoreline changes due to Hurricane Sandy, modeling coastal change scenarios, and restoring sand deposits on the south island of the Chandeleur Islands.
- Landscape Conservation Cooperatives (LCC)
  - Develop adaptation strategies that identify alternative management approaches for identified conservation priorities
  - Produce spatially-explicit conservation designs that reflect the ability of current and future landscapes to support priority resources.
  - Deliver decision support information and tools to various decision makers that influence landscape conditions relevant to priority resources.
- Support for Energy Resource Planning
  - Integrate landscape-level perspective into energy resource planning for:
    - Desert Renewable Energy Conservation Plan developed with mitigation strategies for the Western Solar Energy Plan.
    - Conventional energy siting through development of Master Leasing Plans by BLM.
    - Transmission Planning for BLM to revise its "Section 368" corridor study.
    - Development of a BLM "Planning 2.0" framework allowing for more effective response to environmental and social changes at multiple scales.

OVERVIEW OF THE FY 2014-2018 STRATEGIC PLAN

The DOI's FY 2014-2018 Strategic Plan provides the framework for the programs and activities that are performed by 10 bureaus and multiple offices, and take place at approximately 2,400 locations throughout the Nation.

The Strategic Plan facilitates the integration of programs, the allocation and alignment of resources, and collaboration and coordination with stakeholders to achieve key goals. A set of 6 mission areas, 24 goals, 38 strategies, and 117 performance measures will guide the DOI's activities for the next 4 years. These mission areas reflect the Secretary of the Interior's priorities, while the goals and strategies describe the means by which those priorities will be achieved.

The mission areas, goals, and strategies that compose the Strategic Plan are displayed in the Strategic Plan Framework , followed by a description of the mission areas, goals, and strategic objectives, and performance measures. An FY 2018 goal is provided for each performance measure that reflects a desirable annual level of achievement that DOI aspires to by FY 2018 assuming the availability of a reasonable level of resources. The anticipated level of performance for these measures on an annual basis beginning in FY 2014 in consideration of actual resource levels will be reported in the DOI's Annual Performance Plan and Report, that is released with the FY 2015 President's budget and available at www.doi.gov/bpp.

The Strategic Plan was developed based on collaboration among personnel of the DOI, in collaboration with tribes and other stakeholders. There is a high degree of continuity of performance measures from the FY2011-2016 Strategic Plan, in order to ensure an ongoing ability to gage trends in performance and assist decision makers to assess the likely impact of program changes. Trends in performance related to funding and programmatic plans are available in the DOI's FY 2014 Annual Performance Plan and Report available at www.doi.gov/bpp.

Mission Area 1 Celebrating and Enhancing America's Great Outdoors

Goal 1: Protect America's Landscapes
- Improve land and water health by managing wetlands, uplands, and riparian areas
- Sustain fish, wildlife, and plant species
- Manage wildland fire for landscape resiliency, strengthen the ability of communities to protect against fire, and provide for public and firefighter safety in wildfire response

Goal 2: Protect America's Cultural and Heritage Resources
- Protect cultural and historical assets and related resources

Goal 3: Enhance Recreation and Visitor Experience
- Enhance the enjoyment and appreciation of our natural and cultural heritage

Mission Area 2 Strengthening Tribal Nations and Insular Communities

Goal 1: Meet Our Trust, Treaty, and Other Responsibilities to American Indians and Alaska Natives
- Protect reserved Indian treaty and subsistence rights
- Fulfill fiduciary trust

Goal 2: Improve the Quality of Life in Tribal and Native Communities
- Support self-governance and self-determination
- Create economic opportunity
- Strengthen Indian education
- Make communities safer

Goal 3: Empower Insular Communities
- Improve quality of life
- Create economic opportunity
- Promote efficient and effective governance

Mission Area 3 Powering Our Future and Responsible Use of the Nation's Resources

Goal 1: Secure America's Energy Resources
- Ensure environmental compliance and safety of energy development activities
- Develop renewable energy potential
- Manage conventional energy development
- Account for energy revenue

Goal 2: Sustainably Manage Timber, Forage, and Non-Energy Minerals
- Manage timber and forest product resources
- Provide for sustainable forage and grazing
- Manage non-energy mineral development

Mission Area 4 Engaging the Next Generation

Goal 1: Create new, systemic opportunities for outdoor play
- Develop or enhance outdoor recreation partnerships that provide outdoor play

Goal 2: Provide educational opportunities
- Reach the Nation's K-12 population

Goal 3: Provide volunteers on public lands
- Enable the ability to engage more young volunteers

Goal 4: Develop the next generation of lifelong conservation stewards and ensure our own skilled and diverse workforce pipeline
- Provide conservation work and training opportunities for young people

Mission Area 5 Ensuring Healthy Watersheds and Sustainable, Secure Water Supplies

Goal 1: Manage Water and Watersheds for the 21st Century

- ➤ Improve reliability of water delivery
- ➤ Better ensure the future of watersheds against the impacts of climate change

Goal 2: Extend Water Supplies Through Conservation

- ➤ Expand water conservation capabilities

Goal 3: Availability of Water to Tribal Communities

- ➤ Protect tribal water rights
- ➤ Improve infrastructure and operational efficiency of tribal water facilities

Mission Area 6 Building a Landscape-level Understanding of Our Resources

Goal 1: Provide Shared Landscape-Level Management and Planning Tools

- ➤ Ensure the use of landscape-level capabilities and mitigation actions

Goal 2: Provide Science to Understand, Model and Predict Ecosystem, Climate and Land Use Change

- ➤ Identify and predict ecosystem changes at targeted and landscape-levels (biota, land cover, and Earth and ocean systems)
- ➤ Assess and forecast climate change and its effects

Goal 3: Provide Scientific Data to Protect, Instruct, and Inform Communities

- ➤ Monitor and assess natural hazard risk and resilience
- ➤ Provide environmental health to guide decisionmaking

Goal 4: Provide Water and Land Data to Customers

- ➤ Monitor and assess water availability and quality
- ➤ Generate geologic maps
- ➤ Assess national and international energy and mineral resources

DESCRIPTION OF MISSION AREAS

(WITH SUPPORTING GOALS, STRATEGIES, AND PERFORMANCE MEASURES)

MISSION AREA 1 CELEBRATING AND ENHANCING AMERICA'S GREAT OUTDOORS

GOAL #1 Protect America's Landscapes

We will ensure that America's natural endowment – America's Great Outdoors – is protected for the benefit and enjoyment of current and future generations. Through collaborative, community-driven efforts, and outcome-focused investment, we will work to preserve and enhance rural landscapes, urban parks and rivers, important ecosystems, and essential wildlife habitat.

STRATEGY #1 Improve land and water health by managing the wetlands, uplands, and riparian areas that comprise our national parks, wildlife refuges, and BLM lands.

The Bureau of Land Management, the Fish and Wildlife Service, the National Park Service, and the Bureau of Reclamation are stewards of the lands and waters managed by the Department. These Bureaus maintain and restore uplands, wetlands, and streams through efforts that include controlling invasive plants and animals, restoring land to a condition that is self-sustaining, and ensuring that habitats support healthy fish and wildlife populations. The DOI's Natural Resource Damage Assessment and Restoration program works with the bureaus to assess the impacts of oil spills and hazardous waste sites and coordinates restoration efforts.

Annually, Bureaus administer resource protection programs on more than 400 million acres of upland, wetland, and aquatic lands within their jurisdiction. Many of these lands have special status as national parks, seashores, monuments, wildlife refuges, wilderness areas, or wild and scenic rivers. They are protected because of their important and often unique ecological characteristics, physical geography, or historical features. The DOI manages these lands on a landscape-scale basis because of increasing stressors such as climate change, habitat fragmentation, exotic invasive species, and other broadly influencing factors. The DOI also works in partnership with others by providing and leveraging resources for conservation activities on non-Federal lands.

Bureaus Reporting	Supporting Performance Measures	2013 Actual	2018 Goal
BLM, FWS, NPS	Percent of DOI acres that have achieved desired conditions where condition is known and as specified in management plans.	325 million DOI managed acres (74%)	335 million DOI managed acres (76%)
BLM, FWS	Percent of DOI riparian (stream/shoreline) miles that have achieved desired condition where condition is known and as specified in management plans.	444 thousand DOI managed stream/shoreline miles (94%)	444 thousand DOI managed stream/shoreline miles (94%)
BLM, BOR, FWS, NPS	Percent of baseline acres infested with invasive plant species that are controlled.	330 thousand acres controlled (1%)	350 thousand acres controlled (1%)
FWS, NPS	Percent of invasive animal species populations that are controlled.	298 invasive animal populations controlled (10%)	409 invasive animal populations controlled (14%)
OSMRE	Number of Federal, tribal, and private land and surface water acres reclaimed or mitigated from the effects of natural resource degradation from past coal mining.	11,347 acres reclaimed	14,000 acres reclaimed
FWS, BOR	Number of non-DOI acres restored, including through partner-ships, as specified in plans or agreements that involve DOI.	640,000 non-DOI acres restored (annual avg excluding AK)	640,000 non-DOI acres restored (annual avg excluding AK)

FWS	Number of non-DOI acres managed or protected to achieve desired condition, including through partnerships, as specified in plans or agreements that involve DOI.	1.7 million non-DOI acres managed (annual avg excluding AK)	1.7 million non-DOI acres managed (annual avg excluding AK)
FWS	Number of non-DOI riparian (stream/shoreline) miles restored, including through partnerships, as specified in plans or agreements that involve DOI.	411 non-DOI stream /shoreline miles restored	900 non-DOI stream /shoreline miles restored
FWS	Number of non-DOI riparian (stream/shoreline) miles managed or protected to achieve desired condition, including through partnerships, as specified in plans or agreements that involve DOI.	1,665 non-DOI stream /shoreline miles managed or protected (annual avg excluding AK)	1,665 non-DOI stream /shoreline miles managed or protected (annual avg excluding AK)
All Bureaus	Climate Change Priority Goal = By September 30, 2015, demonstrate maturing implementation of climate change adaptation as scored when carrying out strategies in the DOI Strategic Sustainability Performance Plan	NEW	200 points achieved on scorecard by end of FY 2015

STRATEGY #2 Sustain fish, wildlife, and plant species by protecting and recovering the Nation's fish and wildlife populations in cooperation with partners, including states.

The Fish and Wildlife Service is tasked with the conservation and protection of populations of fish, wildlife, plants, and their habitats. The FWS conducts these activities in partnership with others including NPS, BLM, Reclamation, and state and local agencies. The strategy to sustain species focuses on identifying and implementing corrective actions that will lead to species recovery.

The DOI's responsibility to protect fish, wildlife, and native plants transcends jurisdictional boundaries, and includes efforts that affect almost 1,500 species with special status under the Endangered Species Act and more than 1,000 migratory birds that receive Federal protection under the Migratory Bird Treaty Act. The DOI is instrumental in combating domestic and international wildlife trafficking by improving enforcement of domestic laws, strengthening international cooperation and global enforcement, and helping to reduce demand for illegal wildlife products.

Bureaus Reporting	Supporting Performance Measures	2013 Actual	2018 Goal
FWS	Percent of threatened and endangered (T&E) species that have improved based on the latest 5-year status review recommendation.	48 T&E species improved (4%)	51 T&E species improved (5%)
FWS	Percent of threatened and endangered (T&E) species recovery actions implemented.	24,285 T&E species recovery actions implemented (68%)	24,300 T&E species recovery actions implemented (68%)
BLM, FWS, BOR	Number of threatened and endangered species (T&E) recovery activities implemented.	3,290 T&E species recovery activities implemented (annual avg)	3,463 T&E species recovery activities implemented
FWS	Percent of migratory bird species that are at healthy and sustainable levels.	726 migratory bird species healthy & sustainable (72%)	726 migratory bird species healthy & sustainable (72%)
FWS	Percent of fish species of management concern that are managed to self-sustaining levels, in cooperation with affected states, tribes, and others, as defined in approved management documents.	39 fish species of management concern at self-sustaining levels (annual avg) (21%)	39 fish species of management concern at self-sustaining levels (21%)
FWS	Number of international species of management concern whose status has been improved in cooperation with affected countries.	247 international wildlife species improved	247 international wildlife species improved

The Department's Office of Wildland Fire coordinates fire programs across four Bureaus (BLM, FWS, NPS, and BIA) that manage and operate wildland fire programs along with the Department of Agriculture's Forest Service. The DOI Bureaus deploy strategies to mitigate the effects of wildland fire and restore burned acres, support communities that are at highest risk from fire by assisting in the development of fire action plans, and respond quickly when fire strikes. The DOI strives to achieve a technically effective fire management program that meets resource and safety objectives, while minimizing the cost of suppression and damage to resources.

Ensuring resilient landscapes and fire-adapted communities depends on implementation of a broad-based, intergovernmental, collaborative, and national cohesive strategy to better address the mounting challenges of escalating fire behavior, increased risk to responders, greater home and property losses, and increased threats to communities. The DOI is a lead agency in this collaborative approach with the Forest Service and other Federal, state, tribal, and local governments and stakeholders. Three supporting performance measures were developed to demonstrate and evaluate progress in achieving the national goals to restore and maintain resilient landscapes, promote fire-adapted communities, and respond to wildfires.

Office Reporting	Supporting Performance Measures	2013 Actual	2018 Goal
OWF	Percent of DOI-managed landscape acres that are in a desired condition as a result of fire management objectives.	160,066,449 acres managed in desired condition (36%)	171,310,000 acres managed in desired condition (38%)
OWF	Percent of DOI-managed treatments that reduce risk to communities that have a wildland fire mitigation plan.	1,597 treatments (76%)	1,597 treatments (76%)
OWF	Percent of wildfires on DOI-managed landscapes where the initial strategy(ies) fully succeeded during the initial response phase.	6,330 wildfires successfully managed (98%)	6,525 wildfires successfully managed (99%)

GOAL #2 Protect America's Cultural and Heritage Resources

We will ensure that our Nation's rich cultural heritage and abundant historic and prehistoric resources are preserved for the enjoyment and enlightenment of current and future generations.

A cornerstone of DOI's mission is the protection of America's cultural heritage and resources for future generations and the obligation to honor and protect cultural resources of tribal communities. The Department maintains over 29,000 historic structures among 5 Bureaus – NPS, BLM, BOR, FWS, and BIA. The largest portion of historic structures on DOI lands is found in the National Park System. The Department also protects many of the Nation's most important cultural heritage sites. They range in size from pioneering homesteads to the massive granite carvings of Mount Rushmore. The DOI is the steward of millions of cultural and natural artifacts, including those from the earliest days of North American occupation over 15,000 years ago through colonial and westward expansion settlements to those from monuments commemorating recent heroic events, such as the Flight 93 National Memorial in Pennsylvania. These valued collections tell the history of the Nation. These Bureaus work closely with

Native American tribes, Alaska Native corporations, and Native Hawaiian communities to help ensure respect for and preservation of the sacred cultural sites of our native peoples, as well as repatriation of Native American cultural items.

The Department, universities, historians, and others use America's cultural and heritage resources to expand understanding of our culture. They remind us of who we are and where we came from.

Bureaus Reporting	Supporting Performance Measures	2013 Actual	2018 Goal
BIA, BLM, FWS, NPS	Percent of historic structures in DOI inventory in good condition.	15,390 historic structures in good condition (53%)	16,175 historic structures in good condition (56%)
BIA, BOR, BLM, FWS, NPS	Percent of collections in DOI inventory in good condition.	1,214 collections in good condition (46%)	1,225 collections in good condition (46%)
BIA, BLM, FWS, NPS	Percent of archaeological sites in DOI inventory in good condition.	107,814 archeological sites in good condition (64%)	108,000 archeological sites in good condition (64%)
NPS	Number of completed historic rehabilitation tax credit projects (since 1976)	39,662	43,600

GOAL #3 Enhance Recreation and Visitor Experience

We will encourage the appreciation and use of our lands by facilitating visitor use and recreational experiences. We will support tourism and outdoor recreation—powerful economic engines that bolster communities across the Nation. We will strive to provide visitors with beneficial physical, mental, and social opportunities, including those that result from outdoor recreational experiences.

STRATEGY #1 Enhance the enjoyment and appreciation of our natural and cultural heritage by creating opportunities for play, enlightenment, and inspiration.

About 417 million Americans and foreign visitors traverse public lands each year. The Bureaus that provide recreational opportunities – BLM, FWS, and NPS – are particularly dedicated to ensuring that visitors have the best possible experiences through interpretive guides, displays, videos, and other materials, in addition to the spectacular land, water, wildlife, and cultural features themselves.

In a national dialogue about America's Great Outdoors, citizens reiterated the importance of open spaces and recreation to their quality of life, health, and commitment to conservation. National parks, FWS refuges, and BLM public lands provide recreation experiences that include many forms: camping or hiking; catch and release trout fishing; canoeing; bird watching; biking, swimming, and many other activities. Many water-related recreational activities are also available as a result of Bureau of Reclamation projects. These Bureaus make special accommodations to address the need for accessibility to public lands and to better engage underserved communities, especially in response to the increasing urbanization and shifting demographics of America's population. This requires focused research and close coordination with existing partners, as well as cultivating new partnerships with organizations representing diverse constituents.

By focusing on visitor services, increasing volunteer opportunities, and ensuring access for recreation, education, and contemplation, the Department ensures that the public is offered valuable, high-quality experiences at our sites.

Bureaus Reporting	Supporting Performance Measures	2013 Actual	2018 Goal
BLM, FWS, NPS	Percent of visitors satisfied with the quality of their experience.	94% visitors satisfied	94% visitors satisfied
BLM, NPS	Percent of satisfaction among visitors served by facilitated programs.	95% participating visitors satisfied	95% participating visitors satisfied

MISSION AREA 2 STRENGTHENING TRIBAL NATIONS AND INSULAR COMMUNITIES

GOAL #1 Meet Our Trust, Treaty, and Other Responsibilities to American Indians and Alaska Natives

We will restore the integrity of nation-to-nation relationships with tribes and work diligently to fulfill the United States' trust responsibilities. We will work in partnership with tribes to build stronger economies and safer Indian communities.

STRATEGY #1 Protect reserved Indian treaty and subsistence rights.

The DOI will assist American Indian tribes and Alaska Natives in developing the most effective practices for responsible and successful use of subsistence resources and treaty reserved rights to natural resources. For the purposes of this measure, subsistence means the gathering and harvest, processing, consumption, and use of all wild resources – birds, mammals, fish, and plants – from all the varied environments found throughout tribal communities.

For American Indians and Alaska Natives, subsistence use embodies a culturally significant lifestyle and is an important component of their communities. Subsistence resources are important to these economies and for the continuation of traditions and practices that are a part of these diverse cultures. The term "customary and traditional" is included in the Code of Federal Regulations to describe the historic and current use of wildlife and fisheries resources for subsistence by residents of rural communities.

Bureau Reporting	Supporting Performance Measures	2013 Actual	2018 Goal
BIA	Percent of federally-recognized American Indian Tribes and Alaska Native organizations involved with studies and projects to improve Federal and tribal management of treaty reserved rights and subsistence resources.	17 Tribes supported (4%)	100 Tribes supported (44%)

STRATEGY #2 Fulfill Fiduciary Trust

The DOI has ongoing responsibilities for timely reporting of Indian trust ownership information to its beneficiaries. We will ensure that trust and restricted Federal Indian-owned lands are managed effectively and accurately account for revenues in a timely and efficient manner. The Office of the Special Trustee for American Indians and Bureau of Indian Affairs oversee fiduciary trust activities.

Bureaus Reporting	Supporting Performance Measures	2013 Actual	2018 Goal
BIA	Percent of active, supervised Individual Indian Monies (IIM) case records reviewed in accordance with regulations.	710 IIM case records reviewed (98%)	861 IIM case records reviewed (100%)
OST	Percent of financial information initially processed accurately in trust beneficiaries' accounts.	9.3 million transactions (100%)	10 million transactions (100%)
OST	Percent of oil and gas revenue transmitted by ONRR recorded in the Trust Funds Accounting System within 24 hours of receipt.	$628 million timely transmitted (99%)	$635 million timely transmitted (100%)
OST	Percent of timeliness of financial account information provided to trust beneficiaries.	800,000 trust statements timely provided (100%)	816,000 trust statements timely provided (100%)

GOAL #2 Improve the Quality of Life in Tribal and Native Communities

With self-governance and self-determination as our North Star, the Department will work to restore tribal homelands, settle Indian water rights claims, increase opportunities for renewable and conventional energy on Indian lands, expand educational opportunities for Native American youth, and protect natural and cultural resources in the face of climate change.

STRATEGY #1 Support self-governance and self-determination.

The DOI is strengthening the nation-to-nation relationship between the Federal Government and tribal nations because self-determination, sovereignty, self-government, and self-reliance are the tools that will enable tribal nations to shape their collective destiny. Tribes have also assumed an expanded role in the operation of Indian programs through Public Law 93-638 contracting. Tribes contract with the Federal Government to operate programs serving their tribal members and other eligible persons.

Bureau Reporting	Supporting Performance Measures	2013 Actual	2018 Goal
BIA	Percent of P.L. 93-638 Title IV contracts/compacts with clean audits.	79 compact tribes with clean audits (71%)	138 compact tribes with clean audits (100%)
BIA	Percent of Single Audit Act reports submitted during the reporting year for which management action decisions on audit or recommendations are made within 180 days.	405 audit reports addressed in time (99%)	405 audit reports addressed in time (99%)

STRATEGY #2 Create economic opportunity.

The DOI assists Indian Nations in developing capacity and infrastructure needed to attain economic self-sufficiency on reservations to enhance their quality of life. One critical path is economic development and job creation. The BIA coordinates development of comprehensive tribal programs with the Departments of Labor and Health and Human Services. The DOI offers programs and financial services that encourage start-ups and help position Indian businesses and individuals to compete in today's economy. The Department supports tribal communities in increasing opportunities to develop conventional and renewable energy resources (e.g. solar and wind) and non-energy mineral resources on trust land.

An integral part of building stronger economies within American Indian and Alaska Native communities is developing conservation and resource management plans that ensure sustainable use of trust land. Income is derived from leasing the land for timber and forest biomass harvests, grazing, and farming. These plans are reviewed by BIA to help safeguard the income-generating assets that sustain the economy of communities.

Bureau Reporting	Supporting Performance Measures	2013 Actual	2018 Goal
BIA	Total average gain in earnings of participants that obtain unsubsidized employment through Job Placement employment, training, and related services funding, in accordance with P.L. 102-477.	$10.40 average gain in earnings of participants	$11.00 average gain in earnings of participants
BIA	Loss rates on DOI guaranteed loans.	$28,912 loan losses	$28,000 loan losses
BIA	Fee to trust: Increase in the percentage of submitted applications with determinations.	TBD	1,025 applications processed

BIA	Percent of grazing permits monitored annually for adherence to permit provisions, including permittee compliance with requirements described in conservation plans.	3,387 grazing permits monitored / inspected (24%)	8,943 grazing permits monitored / inspected (64%)
BIA	Percent of active agricultural and grazing leases monitored annually for adherence to lease provisions, including lessee compliance with responsibilities described in conservation plans.	9,154 leases monitored / inspected (35%)	17,078 leases monitored / inspected (69%)
BIA	Percent of range units assessed during the reporting year for level of utilization and/or rangeland condition/trend.	1,247 range units assessed (32%)	2,646 range units assessed (74%)
BIA	Percent of sustainable harvest of forest biomass utilized for energy and other products.	2 million tons of biomass harvested (50%)	3.4 million tons of biomass harvested (85%)

STRATEGY #3 Strengthen Indian education.

The DOI is allocating funds to improve its Bureau of Indian Education (BIE) funded schools, and improve the learning environment of BIE students. Improving performance in BIE schools is a challenge the DOI is addressing through initiatives aimed at increasing student achievement with a focus on reading and math. Schools are assessed for their Adequate Yearly Progress (AYP) which is defined by each state based on judging reading and mathematics proficiency along with attendance for elementary and middle schools, and graduation rates for high schools.

Bureau Reporting	Supporting Performance Measures	2013 Actual	2018 Goal
BIE	Percent of BIE schools achieving AYP (or comparable measure).	45 schools achieving AYP (26%)	66 schools achieving AYP (38%)
BIE	Percent of BIE school facilities in acceptable condition as measured by the Facilities Condition Index.	147 facilities in acceptable condition (81%)	164 facilities in acceptable condition (90%)

STRATEGY #4 Make communities safer.

The DOI will strengthen law enforcement in Indian Country by putting more officers on the streets, bolstering tribal courts, and helping fight violent crime and drug abuse. Crime control, however, is only one component of a safe community. New construction, renovation, and maintenance of facilities, including detention facilities and roads and bridges, also contribute to the safety and well-being of the tribal populace.

Tribal justice systems are an essential part of tribal governments, which interface with BIA and tribal law enforcement activities. Congress and the Federal courts have repeatedly recognized tribal justice systems as the appropriate forums for adjudicating disputes and minor criminal activity within Indian Country. It is important that the BIA and tribal law enforcement activities complement the operations of the tribal courts to ensure that justice in the tribal forums is administered effectively.

Bureau Reporting	Supporting Performance Measures	2013 Actual	2018 Goal
BIA	Percent of law enforcement facilities that are in acceptable condition as measured by the Facilities Condition Index (FCI).	46 facilities in acceptable condition (92%)	50 facilities in acceptable condition (100%)

BIA	Percent of BIA funded tribal judicial systems receiving an acceptable rating under independent tribal judicial system reviews.	77 tribal justice systems rated acceptable (42%)	173 tribal justice systems rated acceptable (92%)
BIA	Part I violent crime incidents per 100,000 Indian Country inhabitants receiving law enforcement services. Safer and More Resilient Communities in Indian Country Priority Goal = By September 30, 2015, reduce rates of repeat incarceration in three target tribal communities by 3% through a comprehensive "alternatives to incarceration" strategy	442 violent crimes per 100,000 residents	At or below national average (387 per 100,000 residents)
BIA	Percent of miles of road in acceptable condition based on the Service Level Index.	5,048 miles of roads in acceptable condition (17%)	5,200 miles of roads in acceptable condition (17%)
BIA	Percent of bridges in acceptable condition based on the Service Level Index.	622 bridges in acceptable condition (68%)	622 bridges in acceptable condition (68%)

GOAL #3 Empower Insular Communities

The Department empowers insular communities by improving the quality of life, creating economic opportunity, and promoting efficient and effective governance. The U.S.-affiliated insular areas include: the territories of American Samoa, Guam, the U.S. Virgin Islands, and the Commonwealth of the Northern Mariana Islands. The DOI also administers and oversees Federal assistance provided to the three Freely Associated States: the Federated States of Micronesia, the Republic of the Marshall Islands, and the Republic of Palau. The Assistant Secretary for Insular Affairs and the Office of Insular Affairs carry out these responsibilities on behalf of the Secretary.

STRATEGY #1 Improve quality of life.

The DOI will assist the insular areas to improve the quality of life by pairing access to financial resources for capital improvements and public services with robust oversight, and by improving interagency coordination on insular issues. We will also pursue sustainable, indigenous energy strategies to lessen dependence on oil imports and provide more reliable and affordable energy. In addition, we are working with other partners, such as the Department of Health and Human Services, to improve the quality of healthcare across the insular areas.

Office Reporting	Supporting Performance Measures	2013 Actual	2018 Goal
OIA	Percent of Community Water Systems (CWS) that receive health-based violation notices from the U.S. Environmental Protection Agency.	28 community water systems out of 148 water systems (19%)	No more than 9% of systems with health-based violations
OIA	Residential cost per kilowatt hour for power compared to the national average.	3X the national average	2X the national average
OIA	Percent of schools in acceptable condition based on specified safety and functionality standards.	701 schools in acceptable condition (37%)	750 schools in acceptable condition (40%)

STRATEGY #2 Create economic opportunity.

The DOI will help create economic opportunity by forging partnerships that bolster tourism and attract industry by promoting the unique island cultures, natural resources, and by preparing the next generation of business leaders. We will pursue economic development initiatives that encourage private sector investment in the insular areas.

Bureau Reporting	Supporting Performance Measures	2013 Actual	2018 Goal
OIA	Real mean GDP per capita in the 4 US Territories compared to the real mean GDP per capita for the US.	Real mean GDP per capita of 4 US territories ($20K) compared to real mean versus national GDP ($43K) (47%)	Real mean GDP per capita of 4 US territories ($24K) compared to real mean versus national GDP ($43K) (55%)

STRATEGY #3 Promote efficient and effective governance.

The DOI will work with the insular areas to ensure that local and Federal funding is being used efficiently and effectively by improving insular government financial policies and procedures, financial management systems, and technical planning abilities. We will also strive to equip insular area leadership with the statistical tools necessary for informed decisionmaking.

Bureau Reporting	Supporting Performance Measures	2013 Actual	2018 Goal
OIA	Number of insular governments with on-time and unqualified single audits.	4 (of 7 insular area governments)	5 (of 7 insular area governments)

MISSION AREA 3 POWERING OUR FUTURE AND RESPONSIBLE USE OF THE NATION'S RESOURCES

GOAL #1 Secure America's Energy Resources

As manager of one-fifth of the Nation's landmass and energy resources on 1.7 billion acres of the Outer Continental Shelf (OCS), the Department plays a central and essential role in powering America's future through the responsible development of our Nation's abundant domestic energy resources. Through early planning, thoughtful mitigation, and the application of sound science, DOI can ensure that the Administration's "all-of-the-above" energy strategy includes not only traditional sources, but also the further development of new, cleaner resources to help mitigate the causes of climate change. Included in this development is a reliable, resilient, and well-planned energy transmission system that forms the backbone of the Nation's energy economy and is crucial to bringing both conventional and renewable energy to households across America. By modernizing practices, leveraging technology, and looking across the government and industry for best practices, DOI is improving the transparency and timeliness of the resource development permitting process while providing greater certainty to industry and strengthening inspection and regulatory enforcement programs.

STRATEGY #1 Ensure environmental compliance and the safety of energy development.

One of the keys to further expanding safe and responsible energy development is maintaining the public's confidence that this activity can be conducted in an environmentally responsible manner and is subject to strong oversight. The DOI is pressing forward with a reform agenda, both onshore and offshore, and is bolstering oversight and inspections. The DOI is focused on risk and is appropriately devoting limited oversight resources based on robust assessments of risk.

Bureaus Reporting	Supporting Performance Measures	2013 Actual	2018 Goal
OSMRE	Percent of active coal mining sites that are free of off-site impacts.	6,568 mining sites free of off-site impacts (89%)	6,665 mining sites free of off-site impacts (90%)
OSMRE	Percent of coal mine acreage reclaimed.	5.1 million acres reclaimed (76%)	5.6 million acres reclaimed (77%)
BLM	Percent of oil and gas acres reclaimed to appropriate final land condition.	1,661 acres reclaimed (24%)	2,000 acres reclaimed (25%)
BLM	Percent of producing fluid mineral cases that have a completed inspection during the year. Oil and Gas Development Priority Goal = By September 30, 2015, the BLM will increase the completion of inspections of federal and Inidan high risk oil and gas cases by 9% over FY 2011 levels, which is equivalent to covering as much as 95% of the potential high risk oil and gas cases.	10,204 cases inspected (37%)	10,715 cases inspected (39%)
BSEE	Amount (in barrels) of operational offshore oil spilled per million barrels produced.	<1 barrel spilled per million produced	< 1 barrel spilled per million produced
BSEE	Number of recordable injuries per 200,000 offshore man hours in DOI-regulated activities.	0.3 injuries per 200,000 offshore workhours	< 0.3 injuries per 200,000 offshore workhours

STRATEGY #2 Develop renewable energy potential.

The DOI is working to move America to a clean and sustainable energy future and, as called for in President Obama's Climate Action Plan, will re-double efforts on renewable energy as we transition to a landscape-level approach to wind, solar, geothermal, and hydropower energy development. Standing up new sources of clean energy generation and facilitating the construction of new or upgraded transmission networks are helping to create new industries and supply chains, driving economic growth and job creation. Connecting renewable energy projects to the grid and key markets is central to making renewable energy generation projects viable. Through partnerships and close coordination, the DOI works to site renewable energy projects in the right places where potential environmental and social conflicts can be minimized and potential effects mitigated, consistent with landscape-level planning.

Hydropower is the Nation's largest renewable energy resource, and the Bureau of Reclamation is the second largest hydropower producer in the United States. Our 53 power plants generate more than 40 billion kilowatt hours annually, enough electricity to serve 3.5 million homes. Over the next 12 years, Reclamation is initiating major rehabilitation and upgrades to many of its large hydropower assets which will yield over 250 Megawatts of additional capacity via increased efficiencies. These actions may affect peak availability of units in a given year during this period.

Bureaus Reporting	Supporting Performance Measures	2013 Actual	2018 Goal
BOR	Percent of hydropower facilities in good condition as measured by the Facility Reliability Rating.	45 facilities (82%) in good condition	45 facilities (82%) in good condition
BOR	Percent of time that BOR hydroelectric generating units are available to the inter-connected western electrical system during daily peak demand periods.	85% operational during peak periods	85% operational during peak periods
BLM, BOEM	Number of megawatts of approved capacity authorized on public land and the OCS for renewable energy development while ensuring full environmental review (cumulative since after 2009). Renewable Energy Priority Goal = By September 30, 2015, increase approved capacity authorized for renewable solar, wind, and geothermal energy resources affecting DOI managed lands, while ensuring full environmental review, to at least 16,500 megawatts (since 2009)	13,786 MW	18,000 MW

STRATEGY #3 Manage conventional energy development.

The DOI oversees vast resources that, when developed the right way and in the right places, support "all of the above" energy strategy that expands the production of energy at home, promotes energy security, and helps drive the economy and job growth.

Bureaus Reporting	Supporting Performance Measures	2013 Actual	2018 Goal
BOEM	Number of offshore lease sales held consistent with the Secretary's 5-Year Oil and Gas Program (2012-2017; lease sales subject to change under Section 18(e) of the OCS Lands Act).	5 lease sales held (cumulative 2012-2013)	15 lease sales held (cumulative 2012-2017)
BLM	Percent of coal lease applications processed.	6 applications processed (15%)	6 applications processed (15%)
BLM	Percent of pending fluid minerals Applications for Permit to Drill (APDs) which are processed.	4,892 applications processed (60%)	5,135 applications processed (62%)

STRATEGY #4 Account for energy revenue.

The DOI is committed to providing reasonable assurance that it is collecting every dollar due from Federal and Indian lands leased for energy development. The Department will fulfill its role by accurately and efficiently collecting, accounting for, analyzing, auditing, and disbursing revenues associated with offshore and onshore energy production. Revenues generated from these activities are distributed to states and tribes, fund land protection and historic preservation, and are deposited in the U.S. Treasury.   The DOI also is committed to working with industry, as well as public and non-governmental entities, as part of the international Extractive Industries Transparency Initiative (EITI), which offers a voluntary framework for governments to disclose revenues received from oil, gas, and mining assets, with parallel disclosure by companies of what they have paid governments in royalties, rents, bonuses, taxes and other payments. The Department is working diligently towards obtaining compliance with the international EITI standards and in December 2013 submitted the U.S. Candidacy Application to the International EITI Board.

Office Reporting	Supporting Performance Measures	2013 Actual	2018 Goal
ONRR	Percent of Federal and Indian revenues disbursed on a timely basis per statute.	99% (of $2.5B annual avg 2009-2012)	99% (of $2.5B annual avg 2009-2012)
ONRR	Percent of Payors and Operators covered by a completed ONRR Compliance Activity.	90% (of 3,400 payors and operators)	90% (of 3,000 payors and operators)

GOAL #2 Sustainably Manage Timber, Forage, and Non-energy Minerals

STRATEGY #1 Manage timber and forest product resources.

The DOI's forests or woodlands are managed by BLM for the benefit of the American public. The BLM maintains a permanent source of timber supply, which supports the production of commodities such as lumber, plywood, and paper, while also protecting watersheds, regulating stream flow, contributing to the economic stability of local communities and industries, and providing recreational opportunities.

Bureau Reporting	Supporting Performance Measures	2013 Actual	2018 Goal
BLM	Percent of allowable timber sale quantity offered for sale consistent with applicable resource management plans.	162 million board feet of timber (80%)	162 million board feet of timber (80%)
BLM	Volume of wood products offered consistent with applicable management plans.	243 million board feet of wood products offered	243 million board feet of wood products offered

* million board feet of timber

STRATEGY #2 Provide for sustainable forage and grazing.

The BLM manages livestock grazing on over half of its public lands. The BLM's overall objective is to ensure the long-term health and productivity of these lands. The BLM uses a variety of methods to accomplish this objective – periodic rest or deferment of grazing in pastures in specific allotments during critical growth periods; vegetation treatments; and projects such as water development and fences. The terms and conditions for grazing on BLM managed lands, such as stipulations on forage use and season of use, are set forth in the permits and leases issued by the Bureau to public land ranchers.

Bureau Reporting	Supporting Performance Measures	2013 Actual	2018 Goal
BLM	Percent of grazing permits and leases processed as planned consistent with applicable resource management plans.	1,344 grazing permits and leases processed (21%)	3,500 grazing permits and leases processed (60%)

STRATEGY #3 Manage non-energy mineral development.

Non-energy minerals development on DOI lands and waters, such as gold, zinc, lead, copper, iron, salt, sand, potassium, phosphate, stone, gravel, and clay, support a broad array of uses, including medical applications, computer production, coastal restoration, automobile production, and highway construction and maintenance. The DOI is committed to sustaining mineral development in an environmentally responsible way by ensuring the reclamation of areas that have been mined and minimizing environmental impacts during the mining process.

Bureau Reporting	Supporting Performance Measures	2013 Actual	2018 Goal
BLM	Percent of non-energy mineral exploration and development requests processed.	114 requests processed (24%)	114 requests processed (24%)
BLM	Number of mined acres reclaimed to appropriate land condition and water quality standards.	2,279 acres reclaimed	2,300 acres reclaimed
BOEM	Number of sand and gravel requests processed for coastal restoration projects	NEW	10

MISSION AREA 4 ENGAGING THE NEXT GENERATION

"For the health of our economy and our public lands, it's critical that we work now to establish meaningful and deep connections between young people – from every background and every community – and the great outdoors."

Secretary Sally Jewell
October 31, 2013

The future of our public lands depends upon young people serving as active stewards of the environment throughout their lives. However, there is a growing disconnect between young people and the great outdoors – and it's a gap that DOI has the power to help bridge. The Department has a unique opportunity to harness the strong spirit of community service and volunteerism that is alive within our Nation's youth, and encourage them to use their time, energy, and talent to better our natural and cultural treasures. Through public-private partnerships and in conjunction with all levels of government, DOI will expand its efforts to inspire millions of young people to play, learn, serve, and work outdoors.

GOAL #1 Play Develop or enhance outdoor recreation partnerships in a total of 50 cities over the next 4 years to create new, systemic opportunities for outdoor play for over 10 million young people.

By participating in recreation opportunities on public lands, our youth strengthen their ties to America's backyard. However, nearly 80 percent of the United States' population lives in cities. The DOI can leverage our experience and expertise to help communities engage more young people on all public lands. To increase the number of youth who play outside, we must overcome the major obstacles including a lack of access in communities, a lack of interest from children, and a lack of time for young adults. To address these problems, DOI will develop or enhance outdoor recreation partnerships in 50 cities with the goal of creating new systemic opportunities for outdoor play for over 10 million young people.

This goal will build upon the National Park Service's plan for the Centennial. As part of the NPS Call to Action for the Centennial, the NPS has committed to developing proactive Rivers, Trails and Conservation Assistance Programs and collaborative park-based programs in the 50 largest urban areas and those with the least access to parks. The NPS is also establishing 50 formal partnerships with health and medical providers across the Country.

Bureaus Reporting	Supporting Performance Measures	2013 Actual	2018 Goal
All Bureaus	Number of young people in 50 cities that participate in an outdoor play activity on public lands	NEW	10 million participants since FY 2013

GOAL #2 Learn In 4 years, provide educational opportunities to at least 10 million of the Nation's K-12 student population annually.

Our public lands and waters are our outdoor laboratories, and by getting students–from grammar school to graduate school–to learn about our public lands and waters, we can develop their interest in nature and the science, technology, engineering, and mathematics (STEM) education fields that are essential to our future. There are approximately 50–55 million K-12 students in the US. The DOI currently reaches at least 3 million students a year through its education programs. With new online education resources, we have the ability to reach more teachers and students than those that can come for an in-person visit.

Leveraging the NPS' newly launched teacher portal, DOI will provide educational opportunities to at least 10 million of the Nation's K-12 student population annually.

Bureaus Reporting	Supporting Performance Measures	2013 Actual	2018 Goal
All Bureaus	Number of K-12 students who participate or access educational materials or opportunities provided by the Department of the Interior	NEW	10 million participants after FY 2013

GOAL #3 Serve In 4 years, attain 1,000,000 volunteers annually on public lands.

Currently 332,000 volunteers provide 9.6 million hours of service annually valued at $209 million per year. We know that many more people are interested in volunteering but there is insufficient volunteer coordination and management capacity. By prioritizing volunteer management and coordination positions as part of our efforts to expand youth work opportunities and leveraging the expertise of partners like the Corporation for National and Community Service, we will expand volunteer opportunities across DOI's public lands.

Bureaus Reporting	Supporting Performance Measures	2013 Actual	2018 Goal
All Bureaus	Number of people volunteering on DOI managed lands	NEW	1 million volunteers annually

GOAL #4 Work Provide 100,000 work and training opportunities to young people over the next 4 years.

To develop the next generation of lifelong conservation stewards and ensure our own skilled and diverse workforce pipeline, DOI will provide 100,000 work & training opportunities to young people (ages 15 to 25) over 4 years. In order to achieve the goal, we will utilize public-private partnerships to leverage additional resources and provide additional work and training opportunities than those we could do on our own. Our work and training opportunities will support the 21st Century Conservation Service Corps (21CSC) which is a multi-agency effort to provide work and training opportunities in stewardship of our public lands to young people and veterans, helping them develop skills to serve both the Nation's natural and cultural resources, but also their own futures. The other 21 CSC Federal agency partners are Agriculture, Commerce, Labor, Environmental Protection Agency, Army, Council on Environmental Quality, and the Corporation for National and Community Service.

Bureaus Reporting	Supporting Performance Measures	2013 Actual	2018 Goal
All Bureaus	Number of work and training opportunities provided to young people Youth Employment and Training Priority Goal = By September 30, 2015, the DOI will provide 40,000 work and training opportunities over two fiscal years, 2014 and 2015, for individuals ages 15 to 25 to support the mission of the DOI.	15,546 Participants in FY 2013	80,000 opportunities after FY 2013

MISSION AREA 5: ENSURING HEALTHY WATERSHEDS AND SUSTAINABLE, SECURE WATER SUPPLIES

Healthy watersheds provide sustainable, secure water that is the foundation for healthy communities and economies, but water supplies are challenged by climate change, record drought conditions, and increasing demands. Recognizing the states' primary role in managing water resources, the Department will work as a partner to increase reliability of water supplies, for the benefit of the people, the economy, and the environment by providing better tools for water management, promoting water conservation and efficiency, and wisely maintaining and improving infrastructure. To achieve this goal it will be critical to inculcate these concepts in the next generation of water managers.

GOAL #1 Manage Water and Watersheds for the 21st Century

We deliver water in the 17 Western States for agriculture, municipal and industrial use, and providing flood control and recreation for millions of Americans. To achieve these goals, BOR balances water supply demands, promotes water conservation, improves water management, and protects the environment through the safe and effective performance of our facilities. The Department has a role in developing innovative approaches to meet water needs and anticipate future challenges.

STRATEGY #1 Improve reliability of water delivery

The BOR and its managing partners operate and maintainits water facilities in a safe, efficient, economical, and reliable manner, and assure that systems and safety measures are in place to protect the facilities and the public. The BOR's Facility Reliability Rating (FRR) system was established to score and provide a general indication of BOR's ability to maintain the reliability of its facilities. The BOR uses FRR data, on both reserved and major transferred facilities, to focus on activities that help ensure water storage and delivery for its customers. Approximately 40% of the total facilities subject to FRR are managed by Reclamation's water partners. These partnerships create significant operational efficiencies but will also require close coordination to effectively utilize available Federal and non-Federal resources needed to achieve the stated goal.

Bureau Reporting	Supporting Performance Measures	2013 Actual	2018 Goal
BOR	Percent of water infrastructure in good condition as measured by the Facility Reliability Rating.	274 facilities rated in good condition (79%)	275 facilities rated in good condition (79%)

STRATEGY #2 Better ensure the future of watersheds against the impacts of climate change

The BOR is currently conducting assessments of existing and future water supply demand imbalances in watersheds within its 17 Western States through Basin Studies and Impact Assessments. When completed, these studies will analyze the risks and impacts of climate change to water resources and identify actions to adapt to the potential effects of climate change. To address projected imbalances in supply and demand, the studies identify adaptation strategies, including strategies for non-structural and structural changes. A wide range of Federal and non-Federal stakeholders participate in the basin studies, which are selected through a competitive process using established criteria.

Bureau Reporting	Supporting Performance Measures	2013 Actual	2018 Goal
BOR	Percent of basin studies that have been completed.	4 basin studies completed (20%)	17 basin studies completed (89%)

GOAL #2 Extend the Supply of Water through Conservation

STRATEGY #1 Expand Water Conservation Capabilities

The American West is now the fastest growing region of the Country and faces serious water challenges. Competition for finite water supplies is increasing as a result of population growth, agricultural demands, and water for environmental needs. An increased emphasis on domestic energy development will place additional pressure on limited water supplies, as significant amounts of water may be required for unconventional and renewable energy development.

Impacts of climate change, as evidenced by increases in temperature, decreases in precipitation and snowpack, extended droughts, and depleted aquifers and stream flow in several Reclamation river basins are reducing water supplies. Water is vital for the environment and the economies of rural and urban communities in the west. The DOI will "increase" water supplies through BOR's Priority Goal conservation programs.

Office Reporting	Supporting Performance Measures	2013 Actual	2018 Goal
BOR	Acre feet of water conservation capacity enabled through Reclamation's Priority Goal conservation programs. Water Conservation Priority Goal = By September 30, 2015 the DOI will further enable the capability to increase available water supply for agricultural, municipal, industrial, and environmental uses in the Western United States through Reclamation water conservation programs to 840,000 acre feet, cumulatively since the end of FY 2009.	734,851 acre-feet of water conservation capacity grants approved	1,000,000 acre-feet of water conservation capacity grants approved

GOAL #3 Availability of Water to Tribal Communities

STRATEGY #1: Protect tribal water rights

The BIA water program functions are divided into two distinct but overlapping elements. The Water Rights Negotiation/Litigation Program defines and protects Indian water rights and settles claims through negotiations if possible, or alternatively, through litigation. The Water Management Program assists tribes in managing, conserving, and utilizing trust water resources.

Bureau Reporting	Supporting Performance Measures	2013 Actual	2018 Goal
BIA	Annual percent of projects completed in support of water management, planning and pre-development	36 projects completed (39%)	71 projects completed (77%)

STRATEGY #2 Improve infrastructure and operational efficiency of tribal water facilities

The BIA Irrigation, Power and Safety of Dams program operates and manages irrigation, power, and dam infrastructure. The program sets high standards for maintenance, collaboration with stakeholders, and effective water and power distribution. The BIA manages facilities to ensure they do not present an unacceptable risk to downstream lives and property; and are managed in an economically, technically, environmentally, and culturally sound manner.

Bureau Reporting	Supporting Performance Measures	2013 Actual	2018 Goal
BIA	Number of linear miles of functional BIA irrigation project canals servicing irrigated lands.	3,927 linear miles of irrigation canals	4,570 linear miles of irrigation canals

MISSION AREA 6 BUILDING A LANDSCAPE-LEVEL UNDERSTANDING OF OUR RESOURCES

To effectively carry out its mission, the Department of the Interior must understand and make decisions at the landscape-level. Decisions affecting the siting of energy development, water resource management, recreation, the conservation of habitat for sensitive flora and fauna, the identification of transmission line rights-of-way, mitigation for development activities, and other land uses are increasingly interconnected with one another on an ever changing, climate-impacted landscape.

The Department conducts science to inform these decisions; develops tools to analyze, visualize, translate, and extrapolate science; and is leading efforts to apply it at multiple scales and across multiple landscapes and jurisdictions to inform land and resource planning, policy, mitigation, and management. Additionally, as the managing partner for the Geospatial Platform, DOI can leverage 21st Century Geographic Information System (GIS) tools to transform vast amounts of data regarding our landscapes and resources into useful information to inform decisions about powering our future and ensuring healthy landscapes and sustainable supplies of water.

GOAL #1 Provide Shared Landscape-level Management and Planning Tools

Harnessing emerging technologies, tools, and methodologies, DOI works with partners to elevate understanding of resources on a landscape-level. The DOI will leverage these partnerships and its role as the managing partner for the National Geospatial Platform to turn vast amounts of data into usable information and advance broader based and more consistent landscape and resource management.

STRATEGY #1 Ensure the use of landscape-level capabilities and mitigation actions.

Landscape-level approaches to management hold the promise of a broader-based and more consistent consideration of both development and conservation, as opposed to a piecemeal approach. Over the last few decades, ecologists and conservationists have increasingly worked at larger geographic scales to improve their ability to characterize and combat complex threats and stressors such as habitat fragmentation and climate change. When conservation is planned for and carried out at these larger scales, it is often easier to detect ecological patterns and population dynamics than with conservation undertaken within smaller units of habitat, improving the ability of conservationists to address limiting factors, adapt to changing circumstances, and achieve long-term benefits to species. The rigorous science underlying our landscape-scale databases, tools, and methodologies provides the foundation for a new generation of citizen scientists, professional experts, and organizations to better understand and care for our landscapes. By improving coordination with partner agencies, a landscape-level understanding of resources will be available for these needs.

Strong science based evidence will allow DOI to make strategic decisions relative to conservation priorities and maximize our conservation investments to achieve the best possible outcomes, while learning from our experience and new evidence on changing conditions. Changes in ecosystems and habitats in the face of changing climatic conditions require that future conservation strategies can be adaptive, including the use of vulnerability assessments, scenario planning, and explicit statements of expected biological outcomes. This information can be used to identify conservation targets and objectives that best represent our desired outcomes and then to develop landscape conservation designs, long-term strategies, and forward-looking resource management decisions to achieve them. Implementation occurs using a collection of tools and methodologies including the Geospatial Platform,

Landscape Conservation Cooperatives, Climate Science Centers, and other specialized programs and processes. This information is essential to the successful use of the landscape-scale mitigation approaches being implemented throughout the DOI.

Mapping and imagery tools facilitate sound planning and management, ensuring the functionality of entire ecosystems, the resiliency of species and the predictability of decisions for industry. The Geospatial Platform offers an Internet-based tool for sharing trusted geospatial data. It provides services and applications for use by the public, government agencies, and partners to meet their mission needs. This resource facilitates landscape-level planning by providing a platform for integrated data from Federal and non-Federal partners (e.g., universities, private organizations, and tribal, state, and local governments). By centralizing such critical inputs as habitat characteristics, risk vulnerabilities, mineral resources, energy potential, conservation priorities, cultural resources, water resources, surface elevation, and property ownership, these tools will provide policy and decision makers from Federal and state governments, local communities, businesses, and non-profit organizations with reliable, transparent, science-based information to effectively manage the resources and enable integrated early analysis in a programmatic way.

The National Map, a collection of geospatial data of the Nation's topography, natural landscape and built environment is also available. Updating high-resolution geospatial databases such as surface water and elevation data and topographic map images on a 3 year cycle supports public purposes such as resource management, climate and environment, infrastructure and human services, energy, disaster response, and public safety.

Bureau Reporting	Supporting Performance Measures	2013 Actual	2018 Goal
USGS	Number of communities on the Geospatial Platform that provide information relevant to landscape level decision making.	NEW	TBD
USGS, OSMRE	Number of tools registered on the Geospatial Platform that can be used to support landscape level decision making.	NEW	TBD
FWS, NPS	Number of landscape conservation designs available to inform management decisions	NEW	TBD
FWS	Number of landscapes with surrogate species, including population objectives, identified to support conservation actions	NEW	TBD
FWS, BLM, BOR, OSMRE BOEM, BIA	Number of landscape- level mitigation strategies and actions that provide for the conservation of natural resources occurring before, during, or after development activities.	NEW	TBD
USGS	Percent of the lower 48 states, Hawaii, District of Columbia, and Puerto Rico published as high resolution geospatial databases.	35,789 topographic map cells published (67%)	38,652 topographic map cells published (72%)

GOAL #2 Provide Science to Understand, Model, and Predict Ecosystem, Climate, and Land Use Changes at Targeted and Landscape Levels (biota, land cover, and Earth and ocean systems)

We will support scientific research to assess, understand, model, and forecast the impacts of climate change and other environmental drivers on our ecosystems, natural resources, and communities. Our Bureaus will develop and construct strategies for adapting to climate change based on scientific analysis. The DOI will assist Federal, state, local, and tribal entities by monitoring water quality and quantity; analyzing energy and mineral resources potential and environmental effects of their extraction and use; and analyzing and monitoring changes to the land and ocean environments.

STRATEGY #1 Identify and predict ecosystem and land use change

The DOI will conduct ongoing research to support and inform decisions related to ecological systems for land, water, and fish and wildlife population management. Climate and land use changes are the key drivers of changes in ecosystems, and strategies for protecting climate-sensitive ecosystems will be increasingly important. The USGS uses satellite data such as Landsat to detect, analyze, and monitor changes on the land, study the connections between people and the land, and provide society with relevant science information to inform public decisions. These data are necessary to provide a baseline composite of the characteristics and geographic variability of land cover, such as seen in the National Land Cover Database. Terrestrial and aquatic populations and their habitats are studied to understand their condition and function within ecosystems and provide information to improve management and conservation actions. Managing and protecting the biological and physical components that support ecosystem services and processes is a priority of the DOI, especially as it relates to the impacts of climate change.

Bureau Reporting	Supporting Performance Measures	2013 Actual	2018 Goal
USGS	Percent of targeted fish and aquatic populations and their habitats for which information is available regarding limiting factors such as migratory barriers, habitat, and effects of disturbance (fire, flood, nutrient enhancement).	51 of 118 fish and aquatic populations supported (43%)	60 of 118 fish and aquatic populations supported (51%)
USGS	Percent of targeted wildlife populations for which science information is provided for management decision making to inform and improve conservation.	216 of 354 wildlife populations supported (61%)	240 of 354 wildlife populations supported (67%)
USGS	Percent of targeted species for which monitoring and decision support information on their status and trends are available.	187 of 645 species supported (29%)	190 of 645 species supported (29%)
USGS	Percent of critical science information products available for successful control and management of targeted groups of invasive species.	27 of 60 critical science information products (45%)	30 of 60 critical science information products (50%)
USGS	Percent of targeted ecosystems with information products forecasting ecosystem change.	3 of 9 ecosystems supported (33%)	5 of 9 ecosystems supported (56%)
USGS	Percent of U.S. surface area with contemporary land cover data needed for major environmental monitoring and assessment programs.	354 total path/rows from 2011 dataset complete (78%)	377 total path/rows from 2016 dataset complete (83%)

STRATEGY #2 Assess and forecast climate change and its effects

The extent to which U.S. communities and ecosystems may be affected by climate change will depend on the nature of the impacts and the sensitivity of the ecosystem to the changes. Successful adaptation to climate change will depend on access to a variety of options for effective management responses. The DOI will support research and monitoring initiatives of carbon, nitrogen, and water cycles, and their effects on ecosystems. The USGS will provide tools for managers to develop, implement, and test adaptive strategies, reduce risk, and increase the potential for ecological systems to be self-sustaining, resilient, and adaptable to environmental changes. The DOI also considers the application of traditional knowledge when making decisions affecting tribal communities. The Department and the USGS strategies and measures align to achieve the goals of the Climate Action Plan.

The USGS will, through its existing scientific assets and the DOI Landscape Conservation Cooperatives and Climate Science Centers, implement partner-driven science to improve understanding of past and present land use change, develop relevant climate and land use forecasts, and identify lands, resources, and communities that are most vulnerable to adverse impacts of change from the local to global scale.

Bureau Reporting	Supporting Performance Measures	2013 Actual	2018 Goal
USGS	Number of natural resource and cultural habitat, population, or ecosystem models, assessments, or major datasets developed by scientists and in cooperation with land managers.	10 models, assessments, or datasets developed	20 models, assessments, or datasets developed
USGS	Percent of Climate Research & Development Program products cited/used within 3 years of publication.	354 R&D products cited/used within 3 years (94%)	354 R&D products cited/used within 3 years (94%)

GOAL #3 Provide Scientific Data to Protect, Instruct, and Inform Communities

We will support scientific research to improve the resilience of communities to natural hazards and wildlife diseases in order to preserve the quality of life and reduce the likelihood of fatalities and economic losses. The USGS will lead the scientific research on the environment and natural hazards and provide information to partners and stakeholders for use in making decisions that will protect lives.

STRATEGY #1 Monitor and assess natural hazards risk and resilience

The DOI's monitoring and assessments provide information and the scientific understanding that will help protect communities by significantly reducing the vulnerability of millions of people to natural hazards. For example, USGS, working with many partners, collects accurate and timely data from modern earth observation networks and surveys, analyzes those data to assess areas that are at risk due to natural hazards, and conducts focused research to improve hazard predictions.

Bureau Reporting	Supporting Performance Measures	2013 Actual	2018 Goal
USGS	Percent completion of earthquake and volcano hazard assessments for moderate to high hazard areas.	76 assessments completed (38%)	80 assessments completed (40%)
USGS	Percent implementation of optimal earthquake and volcano monitoring for moderate to high hazard areas.	68 measurement sets completed (34%)	78 measurement sets completed (39%)
USGS	Percent of regional and topical ocean and coastal studies that cite USGS products within 3 years of study completion.	20 studies cited (80%)	20 studies cited (80%)

STRATEGY #2 Provide environmental health science to guide decisionmaking

Human health is often related to the health of the environment and wildlife. The emergence of diseases from exposure to environmental contaminants and diseases transferred between animals and humans is a growing concern. The DOI is taking a leadership role in providing the natural science information needed by health researchers, policy makers, and the public to safeguard public health by monitoring the quality of the environment and wildlife disease reservoirs, by identifying emerging environmental quality concerns and emerging threats from disease transmitted from animals to humans, and by providing critical knowledge that helps guide actions to manage, mitigate, and prevent adverse impacts on the environment, wildlife, and human health.

Bureau Reporting	Supporting Performance Measures	2013 Actual	2018 Goal
USGS	Number of knowledge products on the quality and health of the environment that inform the public and decision makers.	224 products produced (80%)	238 products produced (85%)

GOAL #4 Provide Water and Land Data to Customers

The Department, through USGS, will lead the effort to provide water and land data to customers for their various uses. The USGS will gather and present data at targeted and landscape-levels to advance and refine our understanding of the earth and its geologic and ecologic systems. Three dimensional models of ground water aquifers and energy and mineral deposits in the subsurface will be generated to help identify prospective areas for exploration and utilization. We will produce vegetation maps and data to support and inform risk management of wildland fires, wildlife, and other natural resources. We will deliver high resolution geospatial databases and topographic map images to support public purposes and enhance resource management.

STRATEGY #1 Monitor and assess water availability and quality

The Nation faces an increasing set of water resource challenges. The DOI will continue to monitor and conduct research to generate a more precise estimate of water availability and use for meeting current and future human, environmental, and wildlife requirements. These research and monitoring activities will help identify water resources for use by humans and the environment while also developing tools to forecast likely outcomes for landscape-level planning needs including water use and quality, and aquatic ecosystem health affected by changes in land use and land cover, natural and engineered infrastructure, water use, and climate. State and local governments rely heavily on the monitoring data that is provided by USGS monitoring systems that operate across the Country.

Bureau Reporting	Supporting Performance Measures	2013 Actual	2018 Goal
USGS	Percent of U.S. with current groundwater quality status and trends information.	1,369 well networks inspected (7%)	8,500 well networks inspected (45%)
USGS	Percent of U.S. with groundwater availability status and trends information.	8 studies completed (20%)	12 studies completed (20%)
USGS	Percent of U.S. with current streamwater quality status and trends information.	1,546 site visits (3%)	9,600 site visits (16%)
USGS	Percent of USGS planned streamgages that are fully operational by the National Streamflow Information Program.	446 streamgages fully operational (9%)	666 streamgages fully operational (14%)
USGS	Number of water monitoring sites supported jointly with state, local or tribal cooperators.	18,500 monitoring sites	19,425 monitoring sites
USGS	Percent of U.S. with completed, consistent water availability products.	none	1,056 water availability products (50%)

STRATEGY #2 Generate geologic maps

As the DOI's science arm, USGS produces accurate geologic maps and three-dimensional geologic frameworks that provide indispensable data for sustaining and improving the quality of life and economic vitality of the Nation. Geologic maps and research are foundational for exploring, developing, and preserving mineral, energy, and water resources; evaluating and planning for land management and environmental protection; supporting DOI's land management decisions, reducing losses from natural hazards, including earthquakes, volcanoes, landslides, and other ground failures; mitigating effects of coastal and stream erosion; placement of critical infrastructure and facilities; and conducting basic earth science research. The geologic maps and interpretive products produced through the USGS and its state partners are served through the National Geologic Map Database, which is an authoritative and landscape-level data source for the general public, scientists, and decision makers.

Bureau Reporting	Supporting Performance Measures	2013 Actual	2018 Goal
USGS	Percent of the U.S. that is covered by at least one geologic map available to the public through the National Geologic Map Database.	1,814,735 square miles covered by geologic maps (51%)	2,000,000 square miles covered by geologic maps (57%)

STRATEGY #3 Assess national and international energy and mineral resources

The Nation faces increasing demands for energy and mineral resources, particularly in light of concerns about our dependence on resources imported from other countries. The DOI's energy and mineral resources research, assessments, and information will improve our understanding of resource occurrence, distribution, quality, and supply and foster multidisciplinary analyses of the broad economic, environmental, and societal consequences of resource extraction and use. The outcomes of these activities will inform decision making with respect to such issues as natural resource protection, environmental health, economic vitality, and responsible resource management on DOI and other lands.

Bureau Reporting	Supporting Performance Measures	2013 Actual	2018 Goal
USGS	Number of times USGS Energy Resources Program products were (successfully) accessed online (millions)	4.8 million products accessed	5.5 million products accessed
USGS	Number of times USGS Mineral Resources Program products were (successfully) accessed online (millions)	20.5 million online hits to USGS products	22.5 million online hits to USGS products

APPENDIX
MANAGEMENT
INITIATIVES

BUILDING A 21ST CENTURY DEPARTMENT OF THE INTERIOR

The Department's vision for a 21st Century workforce is one that includes highly skilled and diverse staff reflective of the Nation and is effectively and efficiently managed. Attainment of the Department's strategic goals will be facilitated by the cross-cutting efforts that are highlighted here.

Goal #1 Build a 21st Century Workforce

The DOI's vision for a 21st Century includes a highly skilled and engaged workforce that reflects the diversity of the Nation and ensures that the Department achieves its mission area goals. Success will be assessed through the Best Places to Work rating that is based on the Federal Employee Viewpoint Survey. This measure is strategic and comprehensive and is a nationally recognized measure of the quality and satisfaction of the workforce.

Our organization meets the needs of the Nation, with a significant number of employees and volunteers at the local level and a variety of models for service delivery that are unique to DOI's 10 bureaus and multiple offices. Over 70,000 employees, plus a cadre of seasonal employees, and over 300,000 volunteers perform a spectrum of duties that require highly skilled individuals in unique disciplines able to conduct specialized activities such as firefighting, inspection of oil and gas operations, management of wild horse and burros, migratory bird aerial surveys, wildlife disease necropsy, and others.

The DOI benefits from a workforce that is passionate about the mission, dedicated to public service, highly skilled, and knowledgeable. A workforce, reflective of the diversity of the Nation, is the Department's greatest asset. Differences in background, thought, education, and experience contribute to the varied perspectives in the workplace and create a synergy for higher performance and success in the achievement of DOI's mission goals. The DOI is challenged by factors which include an aging workforce, need for technology, requirement to transfer knowledge, and improving workforce management and planning. The Department is focused on improvement in these key areas through strengthening human capital processes and tools and strategies that can be utilized at all levels of the Agency to ensure the growth and sustainment of a 21st Century workforce. This includes knowledge of current and future workforce requirements, marketing and branding to attract skilled talent at all levels, and ensuring employees are proficient to perform their jobs and managers and employees have the tools and resources required to be successful in supporting the Department's mission.

Strategies for achieving this Goal are outlined in the Department's Human Capital Plan as well as in supporting documents at the Agency and bureau level.

Office Reporting	Supporting Performance Measures	2013 Actual	2018 Target
PHR	Improvement in the National Best Places to Work Rating (Partnership for Public Service), as compared to the 2012 baseline.	Index Score = 59	Index Score = 64

Goal #2 Sustainability of Interior's Operations

The DOI completed its fourth Strategic Sustainability Performance Plan in 2013, mapping out strategies to reduce its environmental footprint with a goal to integrate sustainable practices into day-to-day operations and more effectively utilize resources and protect the environment.

The DOI is complying with the requirements of *Executive Order 13514, Federal Leadership in Environmental, Energy, and Economic Performance* by aligning sustainability goals with mission goals and focusing on strategies to reduce greenhouse gas emissions, build and rehabilitate facilities based upon sustainability principles, and reduce water consumption. The Department's Sustainability Council links the efforts of employees with those of senior management to modify policies and practices for best results such as cooperative efforts (e.g., inviting employees to submit their ideas for improving sustainable practices) that will foster an inclusive and transparent process to promote sustainability.

Offices Reporting	Supporting Performance Measures	2013 Actual	2018 Target
PEP/PAM	Reduction in direct and indirect GHG emissions from sources that are owned or controlled by DOI and from consumption of purchased electricity, heat or steam (i.e. 20% reduction in Scope 1 and 2 GHG emissions by 2020)*	-18.2%	-16%
PEP/PFM	Reduction in indirect GHG emissions from sources including transmission and distribution losses, business travel, employee commuting, contracted wastewater treatment and contracted solid waste disposal (i.e. 9% reduction in Scope 3 GHG emissions by 2020)	- 18.1%(E)	-20%

Goal #3 Dependability and Efficiency of Information Technology

Information technology is a key tool that supports the accomplishment of mission goals; technology can significantly advance the effectiveness and efficiency of programs and help employees to be more productive. Information technology can also help DOI to address increasingly complex challenges in managing a large and geographically dispersed organization. The DOI's vision is developing and providing the right mix of information technology products and services at a lower cost while delivering greater service to employees and customers.

The DOI is implementing a series of technology innovations and efficiencies to deliver improved services at a lower cost, including consolidation of infrastructure and shifting commodity technology services from in-house delivery mechanisms to capable external providers. These efforts will yield benefits in improved sustainability, reduced carbon footprint, and energy and efficiency savings.

Office Reporting	Supporting Performance Measures	2013 Actual	2018 Target
OCIO	Percentage of the 95 DOI committed data centers consolidated.	62% (59 consolidated / 95 data centers)	100%

Goal #4 Improve Acquisition and Real Property Management

The Department relies on the skills and services of the private sector for effective mission delivery, with approximately $4 billion expended annually for contracted goods and services. Over 50 percent of the Department's annual prime contract awards are made to small businesses. The mission goals of the Department are significantly advanced through effective management of contracts in a manner that reduces risk, and achieves desired results that cost less. Through a combination of innovative procurement methods, the Department is focused on the achievement of goals that will leverage purchasing power, promote efficient business practices, and focus on development and retention of a skilled acquisition workforce.

The Department of the Interior's real property portfolio includes approximately 43,000 buildings and 75,000 structures, valued at more than $240 billion, as well as nearly every type of asset found in a local community. Interior's assets are treasured for their cultural and historic significance; scenic, recreational, and environmental values; functional purposes like hydroelectric power and water management; and in some cases the revenues they provide. The Department's asset management program focuses on appropriate stewardship, maintenance, and capital investment for these assets in support of mission goals.

Program achievements are tracked utilizing both industry standard performance metrics and through initiatives to promote cost savings and the effective operation and management of facilities, such as space consolidation and the disposal of excess assets.

Office Reporting	Supporting Performance Measures	2013 Actual	2018 Target
PAM	Percentage of actions processed through existing contract sources (includes Federal Supply Schedule, Government-wide Acquisition Contracts, Indefinite Delivery Vehicles, and Blanket Purchase Agreements).	44%	44%
PAM	Percentage of acquisitions for IT hardware and land mobile radios made through Department-wide strategic sourcing vehicles.	NEW	95%
PAM	Percent change from FY 2012 square footage baseline for buildings predominantly used as Offices and Warehouses	1.5% (E)	4.5%
PAM	Overall condition of buildings and structures, that are mission critical (based on the Asset Priority Index (API), as measured by the Facility Condition Index (FCI)	0.038	0.035

Goal #5 Promote Small and Disadvantaged Business

The DOI promotes small and disadvantaged businesses in the execution of $4 billion in annual contract awards, and awards over 50 percent of its prime contract awards to small businesses annually. . The DOI's program managers, acquisition specialists, and small business advocates promote the use of small businesses; conduct outreach with small businesses to inform them of upcoming contracting opportunities; and provide advice and counseling about the contracting process.

Office Reporting	Supporting Performance Measures	2013 Actual	2018 Target
PSD	Percentage of total prime contract awards made to small businesses.	53%	60%

ACRONYMS

BIA	Bureau of Indian Affairs
BIE	Bureau of Indian Education
BLM	Bureau of Land Management
BOEM	Bureau of Ocean Energy Management
BOR	Bureau of Reclamation
BSEE	Bureau of Safety and Environmental Enforcement
DOI	Department of the Interior
FWS	Fish and Wildlife Service
GPRA	Government Performance and Results Act
IA	Indian Affairs
LWCF	Land and Water Conservation Fund
NPS	National Park Service
OIA	Office of Insular Affairs
ONRR	Office of Natural Resources Revenue
OSMRE	Office of Surface Mining Reclamation and Enforcement
OST	Office of the Special Trustee for American Indians
PAM	Office of Acquisition and Property Management
PEP	Office of Environmental Policy and Compliance
PHR	Office of Human Resources
PIO	Office of the Chief Information Officer
PMB	Office of Policy, Management and Budget
PNH	Office of Native Hawaiian Relations
PSD	Office of Small and Disadvantaged Business Utilization
PWF	Office of Wildland Fire
USGS	U.S. Geological Survey

For further information, visit the Department of the Interior Web site at:

www.doi.gov/bpp

or contact

U.S. Department of the Interior
Office of Planning & Performance Management
1849 C Street NW MS4361-MIB
Washington DC 20240
202-208-1818